Praise for *THE RADIO SIGNAL*

We can hardly imagine what it was like for Christians living in Germany during the Third Reich. But now we don't have to, because my friend Friedhelm Radandt was there and has given us this extraordinary book about his experiences. He writes about it in such a fresh and compelling way that you almost feel it happened yesterday. And unlike many stories from that terrible time, this one has a happy ending, in which God brings Friedhelm through these trials to America—and eventually to be the president of The King's College in New York. What a story this is, and I'm so grateful we can now read it for ourselves.

—**Eric Metaxas,** *NYTimes* bestselling author of *Bonhoeffer: Pastor, Martyr, Prophet, Spy*

A moving account of how faith and love can flourish even in the midst of the nightmare of Hitler's Germany. Friedhelm Radandt provides not only an intimate, first-hand view of decisive turns in history, but a story of hope, grace, and inspiration.

—**Michael Medved,** nationally syndicated talk radio host

This is a gripping tale, masterfully told. Few could tell it as Friedhelm Radandt has. Though a youth in Germany as the Nazis came to power, he and his family never lost hope—a hope that was rewarded in the Radandt's heroic escape and for Friedhelm, meeting and marrying Elizabeth, a fellow refugee.

Friedhelm and Elizabeth have become dear friends. Though we have known them best as outstanding leaders in higher education, we now understand how an awful war forged their character and produced endurance that has distinguished them to multitudes and endeared them to us. We heartily commend *The Radio Signal*.

—**John Beckett,** author of *Loving Monday*,
Wendy Beckett, author of *God Keeps Covenant*

I am impressed with Friedhelm Radandt. I came to know him as I served on the board of The King's College. His and his wife's deep love for Jesus Christ stems from facing and surviving tremendous challenges before and during World War II. He has made excellent contributions to the field of Christian education. I trust their story will be an inspiration to you.

—**Steve Douglass,** president of Campus Crusade for Christ International; president of Cru

In today's day and age, we hear about concerns of threats against religious liberty both at home and abroad. To steady ourselves for the challenging days ahead, we must turn to history for fresh supplies of encouragement. Enter Friedhelm Radandt's *The Radio Signal*—a true story of conviction and faith among religious dissenters and exiles at the height of Nazi aggression. If your faith needs a boost, read this book.

—**Gregory Alan Thornbury,** PhD, president of The King's College, New York; author of *Recovering Classic Evangelicalism: Applying the Wisdom and Vision of Carl F. Henry*

The story of Nazi Germany is of interest because of the lessons we all should learn from Hitler's rise to power and subsequent downfall. However, history books do not tell us the stories of individual families who had to endure the oppression of the Nazi regime. In telling the story of two of these families, Friedhelm Radandt reminds us that behind the headlines were Christians who wrestled with how to live out their faith in the midst of legal and political pressure. Even as Christianity is being marginalized in our own country, this book affirms that amid suffering, injustice, and disappointments, God is faithful to His people.

—**Dr. Erwin W. Lutzer,** Moody Church, Chicago

As children in Europe during World War II, Elizabeth (Job) and Friedhelm Radandt and their families experienced firsthand events many of us have only read about in books or seen in movies: Kristallnacht, the German occupation of Warsaw, the segregation of Jews in the Warsaw Ghetto, bombing raids in Hamburg, and life as displaced refugees of war. The Radandt and Job families were shaped and sustained by their faith and moral convictions. Friedhelm's father decided not to complete the Nazis' Aryan purity questionnaire and refused to enroll his sons in a Nazi training school, placing himself and his family in a precarious position. Elizabeth's father advocated on behalf of the Poles with whom he worked, but he was still named on the Polish Resistance death list. Yet at every turn, the Radandt and Job families sought and saw the Lord's providence time and time again. Though they lost everything they owned, they did not lose one another. As Friedhelm's grandfather August shared with him, 'Even the sad things in life have blessings hidden inside them.' Amid one of the darkest times in our history, their family's story of faith and God's providence, shared in *The Radio Signal*, is compelling and inspiring.

—**Greg Christy,** president of Northwestern College

A treat not to be missed, this book is filled with the exploits of two young children and their families, one in Germany and one in Poland, during the last days of World War II, and their escape from ruthless Russian occupiers. Both luck, and indeed perhaps miracles, and secret faith in covert religion, guide their journeys. Young as well as old will find this page-turner a reminder of times too quickly forgotten by later generations.

—**Eugene Hotchkiss,** PhD, president emeritus,
Lake Forest College

THE RADIO SIGNAL

A TRUE STORY OF A HARROWING ESCAPE
AND A LOVE THAT AROSE FROM A WORLD WAR

FRIEDHELM RADANDT

The Radio Signal

Published by Deep River Books
Sisters, Oregon
www.deepriverbooks.com

ISBN-13 : 9781940269917

Library of Congress: 2016938763

Printed in the USA
2016—First Edition

25 24 23 22 21 20 19 18 17 16 10 9 8 7 6 5 4 3 2 1

Cover design by Jason Gabbert

CONTENTS

PART 3

He who dreads action
More than disaster,
How can he fight
When disaster impends?
—**Max Frisch,** *The Firebugs*

((ι))

The man who acts ideologically
Sees himself justified in his idea;
The responsible man commits
His action into the hands of God
And lives by God's grace and favour.
—**Dietrich Bonhoeffer,** *Ethics*

For Elizabeth.

PREFACE

THE 1920S USHERED in a great boom for the radio, an exciting invention that—once mass-produced—was to transform public discourse and communication, entertainment and news coverage for decades to come. In the hands of a visionary dictator, the radio would prove to be a desirable tool for shaping thought and attitude of his people, and Hitler seized the initiative. Immediately upon assuming power in 1933, Hitler capitalized on this boom when he promoted the affordable, low-cost *Volksempfänger*, the people's radio. As a result, the number of German households featuring a radio more than doubled, and World War II became the war in which news was often picked up first over the radio.

As a nine-year-old in my hometown of Neustettin—renamed Sczecinek once Poland annexed the region of Eastern Pomerania in 1945—I was spellbound listening to the seemingly never ceasing German victory announcements over the Volksempfänger in the early years of the war. It was my dad who from time to time would dampen my enthusiasm with his strong words of disapproval for the Nazis. As I would learn after the war, much to my delight, his actions matched his words.

Toward the very end of the war—I by then twelve years of age and living as a refugee on a farm in Western Germany—the words of Goebbels announcing the death of President Franklin Delano Roosevelt become embedded in my memory. To this day I have the visceral urge to repeat in German the very words and the shrill sound of his voice with which he concluded that newsbreak. Where did I hear

Goebbels make the announcement? It was on the radio, specifically the Volksempfänger.

((ꝑ))

The radio boom of the 1920s affected not only the life of my family in Germany, but to an even larger degree my wife Elizabeth's family, the Jobs in Warsaw, who trace their life in Poland back for generations to the early 1700s when their forbears arrived there as immigrants from Germany. In fact, Elizabeth's father, Ludwig Job, directly impacted the radio boom through his work. Upon completing his studies in physics at the University of Warsaw in the late 1920s Ludwig joined the Dutch electronics firm Philips, at their Warsaw plant, as a researcher and developer of radio tubes, a crucial component for radios in that pre-transistor age. But his work in no way related to what was going on in Germany. That changed abruptly at the start of WWII in 1939.

Given the importance of Ludwig's work to the German war machine, he continued in his research position at Philips under the German occupation of Poland and thus avoided being drafted into the German army. Naturally, for him and his family, the radio took its place as the primary source of information about the war. On crucial occasions, it was news gleaned from the radio that told them when to make their escape ahead of the approaching Soviet Army and which refugee routes to choose.

((ꝑ))

When a few years after World War II Elizabeth and I enjoyed getting to know each other, we discovered that our experiences as children of the war had not been all that different, even though at the time we lived in different countries. Rather, we were struck by the complementary resemblance that overshadows those war years.

Taken together, our stories yield a vivid picture of what it was like for ordinary families, particularly families of faith, to live through Nazi rule and war. The stories of the Radandts and the Jobs during the decades of the 1930s and 1940s create a kaleidoscope of the contrasting cultural and political environments in which these families experienced daily life. They also reflect the ever-growing reach of Nazi power and doctrine into their personal lives, just as they tell of their daring and trusting faith in God.

The many harrowing adventures the various members of these families had to survive makes for a gripping account. Elizabeth and I lived these stories along with our parents and siblings, and we have been honored to share them with many people since. Now, with additional information gleaned over the years from family and friends about the particulars of our adventures, it would seem that a third-person narration, rather than a solely autobiographical account, is the better way of telling this story. By capturing those experiences we gain in historical awareness, and by telling them we preserve their richness for others.

PART 1

CHAPTER 1

((ı))

NEUSTETTIN: JANUARY 30, 1945

THE KNOCK CAME in the middle of the night. It was January 30, 1945, and Friedhelm Radandt was twelve years old. He was sleeping soundly under his feather blanket. The bed next to him was empty. Until recently, his brother, older by two years, had called it his own. But Ernst-August was now stationed in the military barracks on the town's outskirts. Friedhelm, after a long day, was dreaming of where he would take his sled the next morning. That's when the insistent knocking began.

His hometown of Neustettin, nestled in the beautiful farmland of Pomerania in eastern Germany, featured tree-lined streets, a lakeside park, and—most importantly for Friedhelm—gentle, rolling hills. A fresh blanket of snow had covered the hillsides the night before, and for Friedhelm and his friends, that meant sledding.

There was a war on, of course. No one could forget that. Friedhelm's father, Ernst, had been stationed with the German army in Italy for almost a year, and since then the family had experienced a growing sense of uncertainty. Signs of war were everywhere. Recently it had become common to see caravans of horse-drawn wagons rolling through Neustettin's main street, the Bismarckstrasse: farmers were braving the snow and ice of the Pomeranian winter to flee their homes before the Russian army got any closer. Soldiers passed through town too, most of them wounded on the Eastern Front and making their way back home in ambulance trains. Allied bombers were seen overhead with greater frequency, high in the night sky, bound for Dresden with their payloads.

But it's remarkable what a child will accept as normal—and when Friedhelm woke up to the sight of fresh snow, he didn't think about the war. He thought about the sledding. That evening, after a grand time of play in the snow with his close friends Harald and Konrad, his clothes were drying by the radiator. Because school in Neustettin had not started up again after Christmas—due to the front line moving ever closer—the number of children out sledding that beautiful and cold day was uncommonly large, and they often had to wait in line before they could slide down the steep hill in front of the Bismarckturm. Home and warm again, Friedhelm placed his chair next to that of his mother, Gertrud. The two of them were sitting, as they often did, in front of the Volksempfänger—the "people's radio"—to listen to the news. This night was a special occasion: the Führer, Adolf Hitler, was addressing the German people for the first time in months. It was exactly twelve years to the day since Hitler had come to power, and he was broadcasting to reassure everyone with the same promise as always: that total and final triumph was near. "Every wheel," he said, "is rolling toward victory."

Friedhelm wouldn't have thought much of it if not for his mother's unusual reaction. "Liar!" she snapped, slamming her hand down on the Volksempfänger. The Führer's voice crackled and went silent.

Then she sent Friedhelm to bed.

It was his brother's pounding at the door in the middle of the night that woke him. As soon as Ernst-August had turned fourteen, he'd been enlisted, like all boys his age, in the *Hitlerjugend*—Hitler Youth. The leaders of the Hitlerjugend saw immediately that the boy was tough and fearless and sent him for training at the Motorsportführer Schule, or motorcycle school. From there, Ernst-August was drafted straight into the paramilitary Nationalsozialistisches Kraftfahrkorps, the NSKK. Just two months after his fourteenth birthday he was given a motorcycle and a uniform, moved into a barrack in Neustettin, and treated like a soldier in every way.

Ernst-August's job with the NSKK was to deliver orders, including secret orders, to various units and commanders throughout the region. He was good at his job—tenacious—and he knew his way around the county of Neustettin, which quickly earned him the trust of his leaders. That's why, on this night, his commander had sent the boy back home so he could deliver the news to his family himself:

The Russians will reach Neustettin in the morning.

Frightening stories were told about the advancing Russian army, tales of brutality, murder, and rape. British and American soldiers were the enemy too, but they didn't inspire the same fear. The Russians burned and pillaged villages. They showed no respect for human life. They took what they wanted and destroyed the rest. They were ruthless, without mercy and wearing the dreaded countenance of terror.

Friedhelm vaulted out of bed with his heart in his throat. The family had heard rumors for weeks of the Russians advancing from the east, but now it was real. The Soviet tanks had advanced into Pomerania and would arrive in town shortly.

Earlier, Neustettin's commandant had given an order that forbade residents to leave the town. They would stay strong and stay united, even if the townspeople were quaking in their boots. But Ernst-August's commander trusted his young messenger so much that he'd sent the boy to alert his family and deliver them to a public square, where buses were waiting to evacuate a small, privileged group of people. Ernst-August had come to save them.

Friedhelm padded down the stairs and listened to every word his brother spoke as he gave their mother the news. She twisted her apron in her hand while she took in the information, but she remained calm, unflappable as always. Gertrud Radandt had always been a quiet, thoughtful woman, more prone to planning than to panic. She'd understood for weeks what was happening as the Russians marched through Poland and encroached on Pomerania. She knew that her family might need to leave their house in a hurry in the middle of some cold and wintry night, and she'd already packed bags for the whole family.

She slipped through the house quickly, touching Friedhelm's face on the stairs and waking five-year-old Brunhild. The eldest of her children, sixteen-year-old Gisela, was living at an estate called Rittergut Dolgen near the village of Küdde, to fulfill her *Pflichtjahr*, the twelve months of domestic service the Nazi regime had made mandatory for every girl. Before Gisela would be permitted to take a regular job or develop skills for a career, she had to give one year to her country. Friedhelm and his little sister looked up at their mother, wide-eyed, but she kept her voice calm.

"We are going," she said. "It is time."

Gertrud handed each of them a bag, filled with some extra clothing to keep them warm and some food to nibble on, while she and Ernst-August carried two suitcases to the waiting car. They left their home behind them. They left their pictures on the wall and most of their clothes in the drawers. They left the dishes in the cupboards and the chickens in the coop. They left the safety and security and happy life they'd built in Neustettin. And because so few people could leave the town, they even left their friends—the small community of Baptists with whom they'd shared so many sermons, Bible studies, Sunday picnics, fellowship, and food. Mother, sons, and daughter left everything behind.

There was no time to worry about sending word to Ernst in Italy or to Gisela with the Schütze family. Even if Gertrud had found a moment to write letters that night, she had no way of knowing where she and her children were headed or how long they would stay. What would she tell them? The future was a vast expanse of unanswered questions. They were refugees now.

Quickly, the four of them climbed into the car. At fourteen, Ernst-August was an excellent driver: even in the worst winter conditions, he could handle the vehicle with mastery and grace. Fearlessly he drove them through the snow-packed streets to the Hindenburgplatz, the town square where the buses waited.

But as soon as they were seated on the bus, Gertrud remembered the bag she had packed for her husband. In their hurry to evacuate, they had forgotten to bring it along.

"Your father's suitcase," she murmured. "We cannot leave it behind."

Gertrud didn't know if the Radandts would ever return to Neustettin or how much of the town would even survive the onslaught of the oncoming Russian soldiers. Their house would almost certainly be looted, or worse. If Ernst were going to have any personal effects when he returned from the war, they would have to go back for that suitcase.

The officer in charge at the Hindenburgplatz assured her that, despite the apparent rush, they still had plenty of time. "A couple of hours, at least," he told her. "The buses won't be leaving town anytime soon."

Gertrud turned to Friedhelm. "I need you to go back for the case."

Feeling a rush of fear mingled with excitement coming over him, Friedhelm nodded, eager to retrace his steps along the path he knew so well, eager too to retrieve his sled. He was loyal to his mother, ever attuned to her needs. In brighter times he had often helped her in the kitchen, baking the cakes and pies and breads the family loved. And on this night, he wanted to make her happy.

He hopped out of the bus and started half-walking, half-running back to his home.

It was an unusually cold night. The wind blew through his bones as he made his way through the deserted streets of Neustettin, back to his childhood house to retrieve his father's suitcase. It was such a beautiful house, only a block from the lake, which he could see from their balcony. A few weeks ago the Christmas tree had decorated the living room, and the advent wreath on the dining room table with its four candles had made them talk about joy and peace. He missed his dad's presence, but Ernst's car at least was still parked in the garage. The moonlit night gave Friedhelm a sense of safety, and he bounced up the four steps to the front door.

Taking out the key that his mother had given him, his hand lingered on the doorknob as he realized this might be the last time he ever stepped inside his home. He remembered the rabbits and the chickens in their coop and worried about them. Would they die in there from the cold? Would the Russians serve them up for a hearty victory feast?

He remembered too that only a few days earlier his mother had handed him the Nazi flag with the request that he would hide it somewhere so that should the Russians come into the house, they would not find it. She did not want future residents of the house to think that the family living there had been Nazis. Not knowing how to deal with the flag, Friedhelm had taken it and hidden it in the sawdust between the boards of the outer wall of the chicken coop.

He found the suitcase exactly where his mother had said it would be: pressed against the wall in his parents' bedroom. It was heavy, and he dragged it through the house, scuffing the wood floor. Normally his mother would have scolded him, but he wouldn't be scolded now. She would never see that floor again.

Back outside in the bitter cold, Friedhelm pulled the suitcase onto his sled—the same sled he'd been riding all afternoon—and pulled it behind him back through town, across the snow and ice.

The town was quiet: no people on the streets, no planes overhead. Everyone was either asleep, ignorant of what was to come, or hiding because they feared it.

The wind picked up. He bundled up his coat, pulled on his

Fausthandschuhe, his mittens, and began to imagine how comfortable the bus would be compared to this winter night.

Thoughts of the bus made him a little fearful. Where would the bus take them? What would become of his family? At least he wasn't alone. The war had a way of ripping families apart, and Friedhelm was thankful to at least have his mother, brother, and younger sister close. If not for his faith, he would have considered himself lucky. But Friedhelm knew there was no such thing as luck. In this world of war and hope, there were only miracles.

But when Friedhelm turned the corner into the Hindenburgplatz, he didn't find a miracle. The square was empty and utterly silent. The icy, deserted street glistened in the moonlight.

The buses were gone.

CHAPTER 2

BÄRWALDE: JANUARY 30, 1945

AT THE SAME TIME, a hundred miles to the west, Ludwig Job was listening to the radio.

Ludwig, forever wearing a broad and welcoming smile on his face, easily made friends wherever he went. He had a gift for lightening up tense situations, and he was never far from the radio. In more ways than one, it could be said, the radio was Ludwig's life. He'd learned a bit about radio transmission and reception during his study of physics at the University of Warsaw in the 1920s. Later, in 1928, when the Dutch electronics firm Philips decided to expand its operations in Poland, he was hired to develop, improve, and manufacture radio tubes—the technology that preceded the transistor and became crucial during the war. Ludwig had been working on radios for Philips ever since.

He had been recommended to Philips by the man who eventually became his father-in-law, Julius Witt—so in a way, it could be said that radio had introduced Ludwig to his wife, Eveline. But the truth was that the two of them had met through their common faith.

The German Protestant community in Poland had been there nearly two hundred years, but unlike the earlier waves of Catholic immigrants, the German Protestants kept mostly to themselves. In this way they were able to keep many of their cultural traditions, including fluency in the German language and—by and large—their Protestant faith. Most of them were Lutheran.

Only a relatively small number of this community identified as German Baptist, and Ludwig Job and Eveline Witt were part of this small but vibrant community of faith. They had met at the German Baptist Church in Warsaw and had grown close in no small part because of their shared beliefs. Both had decided to follow Jesus. Their faith had inspired them to entrust all of their needs to God through prayer. Now, in early 1945 and having been made homeless by a gruesome world war, they drew on that same faith for strength.

Ludwig listened to the radio for news. The occupying Nazis maintained strict control over radio broadcasts, and the Polish people, for the most part, weren't even allowed to own radios. But Ludwig's position at Philips afforded him free use of them. A Volksempfänger would have limited his listening to the Nazi broadcasts only, but his Philips radio meant that he could pick up stations from other countries as well, including Allied broadcasts in both German and Polish.

It was through radio broadcasts that, ten days earlier, he had learned that the Soviet army was moving west quickly. He decided on the spot that the time had come to evacuate his family from Poland.

Ludwig and Eveline had packed what few things they could carry and with their four children left their homeland forever. Though they had been born in Poland, the Jobs were ethnic Germans, considered German citizens by the Nazi regime and allowed to cross the border into Germany. They fled west some two hundred miles to the town of Bärwalde, a storybook hamlet just east of the Oder River.

It made sense for the Jobs to go to Bärwalde. The town was isolated and far away from places that Allied planes would seek out as targets. Eveline's mother, Eugenia Witt, had arrived there a short two weeks ago, along with Eveline's sister Frieda, Frieda's husband Herbert Rosner, and other members of the Rosner family. They had concluded that

Bärwalde would be a good place for all of them to stay together and wait out the end of the war. As things stood, they were fairly certain that Germany would surrender soon or that the western Allied troops would reach the Oder River. Either way, Ludwig's family was safer in Bärwalde than they would have been had they stayed in Poland and faced the Russians.

The oldest, Eduard, was nine. Georg was eight, Elizabeth seven, and the baby, Waldemar, just three. Though they had been raised as Germans, this was their first trip, as a family, to Germany. How strange for the children to run through town, reading the signs on the shops that looked to them just like the signs they'd seen in their German textbooks back in Poland: *Fleischer*: butcher. *Bäcker*: baker. It was a fairytale place, its medieval architecture lit in the evening with gaslights.

Ludwig and his wife had decided the Job family would remain in Bärwalde, at least until the end of the war.

But that night, right after Hitler's twelfth-anniversary speech to the German nation with its last promise of victory, Ludwig heard a new report on his radio: the Soviet tanks were coming much faster than anyone had expected. The Red Army had rolled through Poland largely unopposed, outnumbering German forces nearly six to one, and they were advancing twenty miles or more each day. At that rate, Bärwalde would come under attack within a day or two.

He thought of his young daughter, smart beyond her years but still so very delicate. He thought of his wife, who was brave enough to face anything but couldn't completely mask her fear so that it didn't show in her eyes. He thought of his three boys, full of boundless curiosity and questions—and how easily their youthful innocence could be ripped apart by the advancing Russian army.

There was no time to waste. Ludwig and his family had to flee again.

After making sure that the doors to the rooms where the children were sleeping were closed tightly, he brewed two cups of *Ersatzkaffee*—hot water poured over roasted grain, a poor substitute for real coffee but as close as they could get during the years of war rationing—and gave one of them to Eveline. Their temporary apartment was unusually small, but for now it would do. They even had found this afternoon some coal to keep the place heated for the next few weeks, and they were now seated in the tiny kitchen by the fire. The plan had been for Ludwig to take the train to Hamburg in a day or two and show up there for work at Philips. That was why his words, spoken slowly, surprised Eveline: "It is not safe here. Not for you, not for the children. I want you all to come with me to Hamburg."

"Hamburg?" She tried to contain her alarm. They both knew the Allied bombing raids in Hamburg had been severe.

"It's our only option," he answered. "There really is nowhere else for us to go." It was an obvious choice for them: Ludwig's employer, Philips, had substantial operations based in Hamburg, and he'd been there several times for meetings. The firm would be able to welcome them there and offer them refuge. Even with bombs dropping from the sky, it was safer than staying put and facing the Russians.

Eveline drank her *Ersatzkaffee* in silence. Finally, she said, "Then we will go to Hamburg, and may God protect us."

Before going to bed, Ludwig went over to the Rosners to tell them of their decision and to urge them to leave Bärwalde as well. They agreed.

Very early the next morning, under grey skies, Ludwig and Eveline with their four children followed the cobblestone road to the train station to buy tickets for Hamburg. Even with the Russian invasion imminent, the train station was very orderly and typically German. The conductors calmly instructed the Jobs to label any luggage they couldn't carry by hand, particularly the big canvas-wrapped bundle that held their quilts, pillows, and blankets. That big bundle would be stowed on the freight car at the end of the train in accordance with a luggage policy that had been in place for as long as anyone could remember. The dire war situation did not seem to have changed either the behavior of the rail operators or their service. But what were the chances that separately sent freight would actually make it to Hamburg?

Ludwig, Eveline, and the four children boarded the seven o'clock morning train out of Bärwalde. The train would not take them to Hamburg—because of Allied bombing, no one knew precisely *where* it was headed—but they knew it was headed out, and they took it.

Ludwig sat with baby Waldemar on his lap, trying to calm his son and his own jangled nerves by pointing out the window and naming things. "*Baum,*" he said, pointing at a tree. "*Baum!*" shouted Waldemar happily.

"*Kuh,*" said Ludwig when a large cow lumbered past.

"*Kuh!*" cried Waldemar.

Georg and Eduard sat side by side, as per usual, scribbling down the name of each town they passed through. They were still in awe of traveling through the German countryside. "*Stettin,*" they said to their brother.

"*Stettin,*" Waldemar echoed back.

But as seven-year-old Elizabeth stared out the window, she was thinking more about people than about animals and geography. Oma, her grandmother, had hugged her so tightly last night that she felt certain something was wrong. When her grandmother finally released her, Elizabeth had noticed the tears streaming down her cheeks.

She did not fully understand what was happening. She knew there was a war going on, though she and her siblings had been shielded from the worst of it. But there was tension in the air. The last few months had been full of grown-ups saying and doing strange things, speaking in hushed voices to one another, and when she asked them what was wrong, mostly they gave her terse smiles and coy replies. "We'll tell you," they'd say, "when you need to know."

Now, sitting on the train with her family and heading deeper into Germany, she wanted her questions answered. She tugged on Mama's arm. "Where's Oma? Why isn't she on the train?"

"Soon, darling. They'll be coming soon."

Their relatives—the Rosners and Oma Witt—had not made the train that morning. It had taken them a little longer to gather up their things, so they had told the Jobs to head to the station without them and assured everyone they'd catch a later train.

None of them realized at the time that there would be no later train. The 7:00 a.m. was the last train out of Bärwalde.

The Job family was one of the last to escape before the Russian army closed in.

CHAPTER 3

POMERANIA: 1934–1937

BEFORE ALL THAT—before the tanks rumbled through the streets, before the bombs rained down on cities and reduced them to fiery ruin, before the armies of both sides swelled to unprecedented numbers and collided and then killed one another on the fields of Russia and Germany and France, before millions of innocent families across the continent were forced to flee from their homes, before chaos was unleashed and life was changed forever—Ernst Radandt was filling out paperwork.

Thirty-seven-year-old Ernst was tall and handsome, personable in his relationships. He had a winsome smile. His love for cars and motorcycles had brought him like-minded friends. Paperwork was nothing new to him. It had been one of the few constants in his life. But this paperwork was different from the rest.

As a boy of fourteen, Ernst had left his home village of Damsdorf at the outskirts of Bütow in order to become an *Eleve*, an agricultural apprentice on a Pomeranian farming estate. As a part of his training, he needed to keep track of which seeds were put into the ground and when, how long it took the crops to grow, and their yield and sale price at harvest. He tracked the animals too: how many there were and which kind, how much they ate, when they were born, when they died, and when they were sold or slaughtered. Farming, it turned out, required a surprising amount of record-keeping.

During his time as an Eleve, Ernst lived in the estate manor house and had a regular place at the owner's formal dinner table. There he learned to converse about the issues of the day—soldiering and politics, mainly—with the estate's neighbors and the many visitors who passed through. Thus Ernst was able to learn not only agriculture but culture too—a valuable apprenticeship indeed.

When he turned eighteen, he was drafted to fight in the Great War. The year was 1918, and Ernst was trained as a foot soldier in the German army and then sent to France. But the war ended shortly after, and Ernst moved in with a cousin in Potsdam, near Berlin. He spent several years there working with a travel company called Mitropa, which specialized in luxury train cars with private cabins for overnight travelers. But the economic meltdown during those turbulent post-war years didn't allow Germans much opportunity for luxury travel. The business was forced to downsize considerably, and Ernst needed to find work.

In the 1920s he returned to Pomerania, the land he considered his home, and used his education in agriculture to secure a position as a government dairy inspector. He was tasked with traveling between the region's many estate farms to look over the procedures that each one used for milk production and to keep records for quality control—in other words, paperwork.

It was while on the job one evening, strolling across a Pomeranian estate, that Ernst heard a young woman singing from an open second-story window. The song was a beautiful hymn he knew well from his Baptist church in Bütow. He waited for her to finish before letting her know she'd had an audience. "What's your name?" he called up to her.

"I'm Gertrud," she answered. "Gertrud Rattunde."

Maybe he had some sort of premonition, or at least a glimmer of hope, that Gertrud Rattunde would someday be his wife.

He lingered under her window and invited her to come down. They talked long into the night.

Gertrud was from the coastal resort town of Kolberg, the county seat. Her parents were still there, in a house just a few minutes from the Baltic Sea's beautiful beach, but Gertrud had come inland to this estate, where she lived and worked in order to learn the art of fine Pomeranian cooking.

"I'd like to try it sometime," Ernst told her—her cooking, that is.

As he'd guessed from her singing, she too was a Baptist—a very rare finding in the mostly Lutheran country. Her father, August Rattunde, had apprenticed as a cabinetmaker but went on to make a career of civil service, first as a mail carrier and later as a postal administrator. He had discovered the Baptist faith as a soldier on the Western Front in France during the Great War.

"Immediately upon professing his faith in Christ," Gertrud told Ernst, "my father took all his tobacco and threw it into the stove. He poured all his alcohol down the drain. The other soldiers were furious, as you can imagine! Then he posed for a photo with the local Baptist pastor and a couple of fellow soldiers and sent it back to his hometown as a picture postcard with a handwritten note that read, 'My Prayer Team.' He was announcing in no uncertain terms his resignation from the Lutheran congregation in his hometown in order to become a Baptist. It caused quite a stir at the time."

Her father had gone on to become a popular lay preacher and member of the Baptist church in Kolberg, and Gertrud eventually followed her father and was baptized by immersion, joining the Baptist faith.

Ernst and Gertrud continued to see one another, and their romance quickly blossomed. In 1926, the two of them were married in the Baptist church in Kolberg.

Ernst kept his job as a dairy inspector, but the couple moved from the village of Drosedow to a small house on the outskirts of Gross-Jestin.

It was a modest and simple house, with enough land for a vegetable garden and some chickens, only two houses up from Gertrud's brother Max and his bakery and just a dozen miles from Gertrud's parents and the Kolberg church. The house in Gross-Jestin, with its inviting slanted ceilings in the two rooms upstairs, was a great house for raising a family, and that is what they did. Their daughter Gisela was born in 1928; Ernst-August followed in 1930 and Friedhelm in 1932.

Three months after Friedhelm's birth, on January 30, 1933, German president Paul von Hindenburg appointed a new chancellor to lead his cabinet: the popular leader of the National Socialist German Workers Party, a man named Adolf Hitler. The Nazi Party had come into power.

National Socialism had been spreading like wildfire through Germany, perhaps nowhere faster or more deeply than in the province of Pomerania. Before 1928, only 1.5 percent of Pomeranians supported National Socialism. But by 1930 that number had jumped to 24.3 percent, and by 1933 it was 56.3 percent. Throughout the rest of Europe, and even in parts of Germany, many people still believed that Hitler's ideas would not appeal to the majority of Germans. But obviously the people in Pomerania felt quite differently.

The treaties that had ended the Great War had crippled the German economy and led to steep inflation that drove the agricultural provinces into terrible debt, and the people of those provinces embraced National Socialism as their best opportunity to rebuild the nation and its economy.

One such plan for rebuilding the economy was called *Kraft durch Freude*—"Strength Through Joy." KdF was an organization that encouraged Germans of all classes to engage in leisure activities—to go to concerts, make day trips, and take planned vacations. KdF was especially keen on making sure everyone saved enough money to purchase a Volksempfänger so that Hitler and the Nazi Party could reach into the homes of as many Germans as possible. Of course the manifest goal of KdF was to cheer people up and strengthen their spirits while also boosting the lagging German economy.

When KdF came to Pomerania, they offered Ernst a part-time job as an administrator. Since his growing family needed the extra money, he took the position.

He was quite successful in the role. He already had some experience in the travel industry from his time in Potsdam, and he was already known and liked throughout the community because of his work as a dairy inspector, so his responsibilities at KdF came rather easily to him. He took to his work enthusiastically and even purchased one of the Volksempfänger radios and brought it home to his family so they could all stay informed about developments in Germany.

Ernst's success at the job drew the attention of his superiors within the organization, and they recommended him for a promotion to director of the unemployment agency for the city of Kolberg. The job would be a step up—more money and more prestige. It would also mean less time traveling to the many estate farms of Pomerania and more time he could spend with his family. It was a good opportunity.

But there was a catch: in order to be eligible for the job, Ernst would have to become active within the Nazi Party.

And so this paperwork, as he sat at his desk with his hand to his forehead, was different.

He stared at it. As part of the application for the job, he was asked to provide a complete *Ahnentafel*, an ancestor table. Thanks to the newly enacted Law for the Restoration of the Professional Civil Service, all public servants within the German government were required to submit paperwork detailing their lineage back through four generations in order to prove their Aryan descent. The document also asked him to describe his relationship with the Nazi Party.

Ernst was not originally predisposed against the Nazis. He'd seen the economic meltdown of the 1920s firsthand. It was a time when he like so many others went to spend their entire earnings the moment they were paid, knowing that a day later the price for bread and butter, for shirts and pants would have risen dramatically. He'd lost a promising job in Potsdam because of Germany's poor economy, and he'd been disappointed by the dearth of good opportunities for work since then. When National Socialism first came to Pomerania, Ernst had been an enthusiastic supporter. He'd gone to rallies to hear the Nazis speak. He wanted, like so many young German men, a chance for a better life, and the Nazis seemed to offer it.

The huge Nazi rallies had the flavor of national and patriotic pride, the first such pride that Ernst's generation had ever had a chance to feel. It was powerful and compelling.

And because the Führer credited God with having placed him in power, and because he frequently mentioned the church as one of the four pillars upon which his government stood, many dedicated Christians throughout Germany saw no conflict between a belief in the Nazis and a belief in the church. On the contrary, it was widely held during the rise of the Third Reich that being a good Christian and being a patriotic German—patriotic by Nazi standards—went hand in hand.

Ernst was also proud of his heritage—at least what he knew of it. His whole life, he'd heard stories of his great-grandfather, an almost legendary figure named Michael Friedrich Radandt. Michael Friedrich showed up at the gates of Bütow around 1800, hoping to work as a blacksmith. A journeyman in his trade, he had left his parental home in the province of Brandenburg and was looking for a place where he could complete his training. He was greeted there by the town's *Thorschreiber*, a government official in charge of registering all of the people and goods that entered or left the city. Within a few short years, Michael Friedrich had a thriving business as a master horseshoe and weapons smith, and he'd married the Thorschreiber's daughter—which made him part of a local family of some renown. It hadn't taken him long to make a name for himself.

Michael Friedrich got married in 1806, which was also the year that Napoleon Bonaparte attacked and conquered Prussia. When the occupying French forces left a small garrison of three men behind in the town of Bütow, they selected Michael Friedrich's home for their lodging, and he was in no position to refuse this dubious honor.

But the soldiers failed to take into account Michael Friedrich's passionate dislike for the French. When they showed up at his blacksmith shop and demanded that he and his family begin serving them more and better food, Michael Friedrich responded by hitting one of the soldiers with his hammer. He then threw the second man into a creek while the third man fled in fear. All three members of the occupation force left Bütow that day, and that ended the French occupation of the town for good.

Michael Friedrich's feelings about the French are easier to understand when one considers that his forebears (who spelled their name "Radant") were refugees who came to Prussia in the 1600s—from France.

The Radant brothers were just four members of a much larger exodus of Protestant Huguenots, roughly half a million of whom fled France because of ongoing violent persecution. The French crown and most of its people were staunchly Catholic, and as the Huguenots grew in number and began to threaten the Catholic base of power, the Catholics responded with more and more open hostility. For over two hundred years, the Huguenots suffered discrimination, disenfranchisement, violence, and a series of bloody massacres.

At some point during the late sixteenth or early seventeenth century, the Radant brothers joined the many Huguenots who made the trek from France to Prussia in search of religious tolerance and freedom.

Ernst considered all this before completing his Nazi questionnaire. His Aryan heritage was sure—but what *was* his relationship to the Nazi Party? He had already been asked to help identify the town's Jewish shop owners and merchants as a condition of his candidacy for the position, after which he was to join a troop of Nazis who would parade these people around town for all to see in order to call upon the citizens of Kolberg to boycott Jewish businesses. That was a side of Nazi rule that up until now he had been able to push aside. Sure, he had heard Hitler put all the blame for Germany's failing economy on the Jews, but living as he was in the village of Gross-Jestin, he had never actually seen actions taken against them.

Ernst knew that his country was in desperate need of leadership that could lift its faltering economy. And he also knew that one did not refuse the Nazi Party lightly. Any refusal on his part could have dire consequences for him and for his family.

But he could not bring himself to persecute the Jews. His faith wouldn't allow it. He read the Bible, and it was clear to him that the Bible's dictates were not compatible with what the Nazis asked of him.

He had to decide whether to be true to his Christian faith or to actively support the anti-Semitic stance of the Third Reich. How was he to reach such a big decision?

If only he could discuss this matter with somebody he trusted. Why not talk to his father-in-law, August Rattunde, a fellow Baptist and radical in his Christian convictions? The two did not always agree, but August had his respect.

The following Sunday, the Radandts drove in their BMW Dixie from Gross-Jestin to Kolberg to attend church, as they were wont to do, and August and Pauline had the family over for dinner after church. While Gertrud and her mother were busy in the kitchen, Ernst took August aside and told him about his dilemma with the Nazis and how it had come about. August already knew of the Nazi boycott against Jewish businesses in Kolberg, and wanting to encourage his son-in-law, interrupted: "I read about this march in the newspaper, and I am very glad to hear that this boycott goes against your conscience, because it goes against the Bible."

Clearly, Ernst had chosen to approach the right person with his questions. "But what about the good Hitler has done for Germany's economy? Does that not make up, at least in part, for his insisting on

Aryan purity in those who hold responsible positions in Germany?" Ernst wanted to know.

"No, Ernst," August replied, "you cannot overlook a moral matter of such big proportions. Trust your insight and go with it. I am thankful that you are considering letting the job here in Kolberg go, and I respect you for it."

There was still another question on Ernst's mind. "Why do those who speak for our Baptist denomination sometimes have words of praise for the new government and even discourage our pastors from acts of civil disobedience?" It was something that confused him. True, the Baptist churches with which he was familiar were free to preach the gospel without feeling shackled, as long as they did not oppose Nazi rule. But where would this lead in the long run? And what would it cost in terms of integrity?

Dinner was ready, and Ernst did not get his last question answered. He did not need to. His mind was made up.

He felt a tingle of fear for himself and for his family, but he had no doubt about what to do. He left the questionnaire incomplete and told the Nazis he didn't want their job.

As for what would come next, Ernst could only put his trust in God.

CHAPTER 4

WLOCHY, NEAR WARSAW: 1934–1937

ON SEPTEMBER 4, 1934, thirty-year-old Ludwig Job stood in front of a congregation of German Baptists in Warsaw with his bride, Eveline Witt, somewhat shy around people, yet full of determination when decisive action was needed. They were about to exchange vows and be married.

A wild, nervous cascade of thoughts crossed his mind as he waited for the pastor to lead them in their vows. He was a serious-minded man, generally calm and clear-headed and dedicated to rational thinking—a scientist, after all. But even serious-minded people are prone to some giddiness on their wedding day. He was excited, happy, and full of plans for their future.

He and his bride exchanged smiles and encouraging glances as they repeated after the pastor. He and Eveline both hoped for children. They hoped to live in a beautiful home in Wlochy, outside Warsaw, in one of the three spacious apartments in Eveline's parents' mansion. They hoped Ludwig would have great success in his career and that this would offer them stability and even some stature in their community. Most of all, they hoped to have a joyful, safe, and peaceful life together. And within a very short time after marrying, they would indeed achieve all of these things.

But neither of them imagined, on their wedding day, while surrounded by their families and their loved ones, that a decade later they would become refugees and leave behind their lives in Poland forever.

The Job and the Witt families had come to Poland by similar paths. In the second decade of the 1700s, at the behest of the Polish crown, caravans of German Lutheran farmers left their homeland and crossed the border into Poland in hopes of finding good land to settle. During the first decade of that century, Poland had been devastated by civil wars, and when the wars were over, the Polish king August II concluded that his country would be well served by attracting German farmers and craftsmen to colonize its unused land and thereby help in the rebuilding of its devastated towns and villages. German farming methods were widely renowned, and these immigrants would bring their know-how to fill a desperate need for food production for the war-ravaged Polish population.

To help lure settlers from Germany, August II promised them the right to found their own German-speaking Lutheran communities within the otherwise Slavic-speaking and Catholic Poland. The German settlers would enjoy full religious freedom and would be allowed to establish their own private schools and churches, just as they would be free to work their own farmland.

The history of migration from Germany to Poland went all the way back to the Middle Ages. Waves of settlers from Germany arrived in Poland as early as the middle of the twelfth century, when a Polish duke asked an order of Teutonic knights to colonize and Christianize the area straddling the Vistula River in the western part of the country. Later, in the fifteenth century, a second wave of German craftsmen, businessmen, and builders were drawn to Poland by low taxes and the promise of free trade.

By the time August II ascended the throne, there was a long tradition of Germans settling in the country, and he appealed to this tradition when he extended his offer to a new wave of German emigrants.

Many Germans responded to this invitation. They loaded their wagons with farming equipment, varieties of seeds, and enough food to get their families through their first winter. They drove their wagons and their cattle east, and they settled the land.

Among these German émigrés were the Jobs, who settled in a small village in Western Poland called Grabina Wielka, just two and a half miles from the town of Dąbie. There they began building a new life for themselves, in the village they called by its German name: Gross-Grabina.

There were numerous such German farming communities in that part of Poland. The residents of these settlements became loyal Polish citizens and contributed to the life of their adopted nation, yet they functioned as a largely self-sufficient social group, characterized by both their ethnic distinctiveness and their economic success. Though they lived side by side with the Polish population, they governed themselves, ran their own churches and schools, and maintained their German ethnic and cultural identity to a remarkable degree.

The Job family did well in Gross-Grabina. They built a homestead that would be passed down from generation to generation, contributed significantly to the building of a new church, and earned a respected place within their community. They were also part of a larger spiritual awakening that took place among German settlers, including those in the area near Dąbie, around the middle of the nineteenth century.

At the time, the Lutheran Church in Poland was spread very thin. Because the German settlers lived in small communities throughout the country, the official Lutheran parsons were tasked with covering very large geographic areas. They did not have much regular contact with their congregations.

Left to their own devices, the practicing Lutherans in Poland started their own revival—a revival that encouraged them to hold small, local prayer groups and to take up more personal Bible study. When a baptism by immersion was performed in the town of Dąbie in 1866, it raised questions in the minds of some locals about the proper form of baptism and about the practice of their faith more generally. Eventually, as a result of this soul-searching, a goodly number elected to leave the Lutheran Church in favor of the newly established denomination of German-speaking Baptist churches in Poland.

In Dąbie, the recently baptized believers opened what they called a "Prayer Room" in 1870. Almost immediately, these early Baptists experienced harsh repression from the German Lutheran pastors in the area, and they had to close their doors. But in 1874 they reopened again for good and began to conduct regular prayer meetings and worship services for their community.

The German Baptist church in Dąbie was here to stay.

It was into this community that Ludwig Job was born on December 3, 1903, at that same homestead in Gross-Grabina where his ancestor had settled upon his arrival from Germany some one hundred and eighty years earlier.

Ludwig's parents, Gottfried and Emilie Grüning Job, were blessed with sixteen children, but only six survived into adulthood. Ludwig was the oldest of those six. The others were all lost to whooping cough or diphtheria. During those calamitous years, Gottfried and Emilie were barred from using either the German Protestant or the Polish Catholic cemeteries in Dąbie to bury their ten children on account of their being Baptists. Rather, they had to use a plot of unconsecrated land that the town had set aside for the burial of atheists, murderers, and suicide victims. It is hard to imagine how they were able to bear so much loss without also thinking of their namesake, the biblical Job, whose suffering demonstrated the profound importance of faith in the face of so much misfortune.

It was his father Gottfried Job, the farmer in Gross-Grabina, who had shown a bend for the sciences. Ludwig admired his dad's knowledge of the stars in the night sky and never forgot how often he had taken him outside to teach him the names and shapes of countless constellations. Clearly, Ludwig had inherited a love for the sciences from his father.

At the time of Ludwig's birth, the largest part of Poland, including Gross-Grabina, was firmly under Russian control. Despite the fact that Ludwig was an ethnic German born in Poland, his citizenship papers at birth labeled him a Russian. But when the Russian Revolution in 1917 resulted in Polish independence, Ludwig was granted citizenship in the nation his ancestors had settled two hundred years earlier.

And it would not be long before Ludwig would have his citizenship changed once more. In 1943, as a result of the invading German army's efforts to nationalize Polish citizens of German descent, he would become one of a relatively small group of people who had held citizenship in three different nations without ever leaving their homes.

During those years, Eveline Witt's family also faced challenges stemming from their complicated national and cultural identity as Germans living inside Poland. Like the Jobs, the Witts had originally emigrated generations ago from Germany, settled into one of the relatively autonomous German communities in Poland, and thrived. By the time Eveline's father, Julius, was born, the Witt family was living in Poland's capital city of Warsaw, where Julius met Eveline's mother, Eugenia Elsner. Both Julius and Eugenia became members of the German Baptist Church of Warsaw and started their family there.

But in 1914, Germany and Russia went to war. As German forces pushed east, the Russian Tsarist administration that controlled Poland began to fear an uprising from the ethnic Germans. The possibility that these people might cooperate with the invading German forces was alarming to both the Polish people and the Russian authorities, and many families—including the Witts—were forced into political exile in Siberia as a result.

Eveline was five when her family was forcibly relocated to the city of Omsk, behind the Ural Mountains. There the Witt children, of whom Eveline was the youngest, attended Russian schools and gained excellent command of the Russian language, and Eveline's father started a successful business as a representative of the Singer sewing machine company.

In time, the Witt family came to feel quite at home in Siberia. They sat with new friends by the tile stove, keeping warm, drinking Russian tea, and listening at night to the howling of wolves and the popping of frozen trees.

On January 21, 1922, the Witts celebrated Eveline's thirteenth birthday, and the question of whether to return to Poland or not dominated the conversation around the festively decorated table.

After birthday wishes had been sung in German, Polish, and Russian, and in the glow of the birthday candles, Eugenia gave voice to her emotions. She had wrestled more with this issue than anyone else in the family. She felt that having to live in exile in Siberia deprived her children of the sense of belonging she had experienced growing up in Warsaw. Speaking in her native Polish, she put the question on the table: "We've been here now for almost eight years. When will these years of exile be over so that we can return to our homeland? I miss Poland, and I miss our German friends in Poland, and our German church."

The outburst surprised Julius. He knew his wife's feelings, but he'd never heard her express them so strongly, or in front of the rest of the family. He decided to coax an opinion out of the birthday girl too. "And you, Eveline. What do you think?"

Eveline, on this, her thirteenth birthday, felt a burst of new self-confidence and did not hesitate to speak her mind—though she did so in Russian, the language in which she felt most comfortable: "I feel at home here, and I enjoy my Russian school friends. They all sang for my birthday today at school. I don't want to change to a Polish school. It's easier for me to speak and write Russian. Why don't we just stay here?"

Julius identified with his daughter's experience. He decided to make his own position known. Like Eugenia, however, he chose to speak in Polish.

"My business is supporting our family and keeping us safe. We are doing well here in Omsk. Maybe we should consider making this our permanent home."

But the political landscape in Russia was in flux, and some eleven months later, in December 1922, the Bolsheviks came to power. The Witts were released from their exile and allowed to return to Poland. Given the political avalanche that a Bolshevik government surely was to unleash over Russia, they decided it would be prudent to do so.

The family arrived home after eight years in Omsk to discover, to their utter delight, that the Polish neighbor who had promised to keep an eye on their house had made more than good on his promise. Their furniture and personal treasures were all intact, neatly stacked in one room and covered over with sheets, exactly as they'd left them eight years earlier.

The same year that witnessed the return of the Witt family from Omsk was also the year Philips opened its plant in Warsaw. Julius Witt was looking for a job after his eight-year exile in Omsk, and the business successes he'd achieved during those years were more than enough to land him a management position with Philips.

Julius used the money he had made in Omsk to purchase a large mansion with several apartments in suburban Wlochy, outside Warsaw, and a second house inside the city proper. It was his dream that he would one day be able to share these with his children and their future spouses after they finished their studies at the University of Warsaw. The Witts had successfully returned to Poland, the place they thought of as their true home.

It was in Warsaw that Ludwig Job first crossed paths with the Witt family. In the early 1920s, Ludwig was a student at the university, studying physics. His Baptist pastors from his hometown church of Dąbie and the nearby city of Lodz reached out to their counterparts in Warsaw, and as a result, Ludwig was given a very warm welcome by the Baptist community there. Ludwig, who took his faith seriously and relished Christian fellowship, quickly found a home with the German Baptist Church in Warsaw.

It was the Witts' family church. Julius had been baptized there years earlier, before his exile, and so had Eugenia. Their whole family attended services there regularly. That is how, in 1925, Ludwig met Julius's outgoing daughter Alma. They had much in common. Alma was also a student at the University of Warsaw, studying medicine, and very active in the church. The two of them began dating and fell in love.

During those same years, the Philips electronics firm began expanding its operations in Warsaw. It added a manufacturing plant and started building a research and development team to explore the emerging technology of radio tubes. Julius Witt knew just the man for the job. He recommended his future son-in-law to Philips, and Ludwig Job was hired as a research physicist, working to develop an important pre-transistor technology.

Ludwig's work for Philips quickly led to notable successes and breakthroughs. He and Alma had plenty of reason to anticipate their future with great confidence, and by 1930 they were engaged to be married.

Then they received terrible and unexpected news: Alma had contracted tuberculosis. She died only months later.

Alma's death was a tragic experience for the Witt family and for Ludwig. Julius bought a burial vault in a Warsaw cemetery, and there, together, the Witts and Ludwig laid Alma to rest.

But the two families had already become intertwined. They continued to work together at Philips and within the church community.

Thus, when in time a relationship unfolded between Ludwig and Julius's youngest daughter, Eveline, people rejoiced, wished them well, and hoped—secretly at first, and then out loud—that the two would eventually marry.

And so, on this day in 1934, they pledged their lives to one another.

"Do you, Ludwig Job, take Eveline Elvira Witt to be your wife? Do you promise to love, honor, cherish and protect her, forsaking all others and holding only to her forevermore?"

Ludwig Job had no way to foresee the dangers, trials, upheavals, and tests of faith that the impending war would bring. Though the Jobs and the Witts cherished their German heritage and loved their German language, their lives in Poland for the time being would remain unaffected by the growing Nazi power in neighboring Germany. Neither Ludwig, nor Eveline, nor any member of their respective families, had ever crossed that border, and even their honeymoon would take them to the fashionable resort town of Zakopane in the Carpathian Mountains of southern Poland, rather than to some town in Germany. There was no way for Ludwig to know how hard it would soon become to keep the promise he was about to make: to protect his wife.

But if he had known, still, he would have given the same answer: "I do," he declared to his wife, his congregation, and to God.

CHAPTER 5

NEUSTETTIN: 1938–1939

THE LEAVES TURNED and fell, the snow blanketed the hills of Pomerania, and the due date for Ernst to submit his job application to the Nazis came and went. He did not turn in the questionnaire that was to prove his Aryan race. Instead, he tucked it all into a brown envelope and locked it away in his desk, incomplete.

His friends warned him that his decision was reckless. "You're not worried about reprisal? Think about your family! It's not wise, in these times, to anger the Nazis."

"It's true, I'd prefer not to offend the Nazis," Ernst answered. "But it's much more important to me that I not offend God."

Once Ernst had wrestled in his mind with the lurking implications of an all-out Nazi state on the lives of individual followers of Jesus like himself, his decision was made. He could not actively support the anti-Semitic beliefs of the Nazis. His path was clear. The enthusiasm he'd felt in recent years about the rise of a new Germany and the idealism that had allowed him to wave the flag for Hitler were both shattered. He knew what he believed to be right, and the Nazis were on the wrong side of it. He would follow his moral compass and honor God's truth, come what may.

The Nazis were still growing in number and in influence. There were more of them than ever on the streets, in the train stations, and in the town squares. Everyone, it seemed, was flying a red Nazi flag or wearing one on their shirtsleeve. And they were becoming more of a presence, more oppressive, not just within Germany, but beyond its borders too.

Since coming to power, Hitler had been aggressively challenging the provisions of the Treaties of Versailles and Saint-Germain, which had ended the Great War by severely hindering the Weimar Republic's ability to rebuild Germany. Hitler dismantled those treaties by violating their provisions step by incremental step. First, he reinstated a military conscription throughout Germany. Then he moved troops into the Rhineland, the area that had been held as a demilitarized buffer between Germany and Belgium. It was as if Hitler were actively daring the other nations of Europe to stop him—and at each turn, those nations responded by doing nothing.

Now, in March of 1938, Hitler made his boldest move yet: the *Anschluss*. German troops marched into his home country of Austria and forced the Austrian chancellor to resign. At the end of the bloodless coup d'état, Austria was annexed to Germany. It wasn't war, exactly, but there was no denying that the Nazis had ambitious plans, and they were beginning to move on them.

In the midst of this, it came as no surprise to Ernst—or to anyone else—when the Nazis removed him from his part-time position with Kraft durch Freude. KdF was a National Socialist organization, and they filled their ranks only with committed Nazis. There was no longer any role for Ernst within that organization.

But his trouble with the Party was just beginning. His friends' worries turned out to be well founded. The Nazis weren't content just to have Ernst expelled from KdF. They also lobbied to have him ousted from his job as a dairy inspector. It was a full-time civil service position, completely controlled by the government—and the government was now controlled by the Nazis. Twelve years of loyal service did nothing to protect him. The Nazis wanted him fired, and he was fired.

Ernst had three children and one more on the way, and he was out of work. And the Nazis in Gross-Jestin had made it clear they wanted to ensure that he stayed that way.

But when Ernst told Gertrud of the trouble, she surprised him. "Maybe it's for the best," she said.

"How could it possibly be for the best?" he asked.

"It's a chance for a new start."

They left their home in Gross-Jestin and moved to the town of Neustettin, and it was exactly that—a fresh start. Neustettin was located on the shore of Lake Streitzig in East Pomerania, some sixty miles south from Gross-Jestin. It proved to be a wonderful home for the Radandts: a much larger house than they'd had in Gross-Jestin and only a few blocks from the lake. There was a garage for the car, a large fenced-in garden, and room for chickens, ducks, and rabbits. The neighborhood was safe and friendly, and the family was able to take walks through the lakeside park and nearby woods and meet their new community. They even started hosting prayer meetings at their house on Sundays.

It was an especially welcome move for the children. The family swam in the lake during the summer and switched to ice skating once the lake froze over in winter. They took trips, when time allowed—one across the lake in a passenger boat to the famous coffeehouse at the Mauseinsel and another in Ernst's Ford Eifel to Bütow for a visit with Oma Radandt. They made new friends quickly and settled into their new home.

But the family's newfound sense of peace was shattered on November 9, 1938, when they were woken in the night by loud, angry voices on the street, breaking wood, the smell of smoke, and smashing glass. It was the night that would come to be known as Kristallnacht: Nazi paramilitaries were marching through the streets with bricks and sticks all over Germany, wrecking any Jewish-owned storefronts, homes, and synagogues they could find.

The streets of Neustettin, like streets in towns and cities throughout Germany, were shining with shards of broken glass, and the town's synagogue was burning. A couple of days later, as they walked past the carnage, Ernst struggled to explain the vandalism to his children. "Some people are vicious," was all he could think to say.

Ernst-August was only eight at the time, but he looked at his father and nodded—as if he already understood so much about the world, as if he already understood that people weren't always kind or good to one another and that's just how it was. But his younger brother, Friedhelm, was curious and wanted more from his father. He wanted answers.

"Why?" Friedhelm asked. "Why are they vicious?"

Ernst didn't know what to tell him. "Be sure not to cut yourself on the glass," he said and pushed his boys quickly past the ruined storefront.

It was days before anyone cleaned the broken glass from those streets.

Ernst wanted only to shield his family from the pressure that was coming from every direction. The German army had already marched into the Sudetenland region of Czechoslovakia. Bit by bit, Hitler was reclaiming the land that had been taken from Germany at the end of the Great War. So far, none of the other world powers seemed to want to cross him; England, France, and Russia continued to acquiesce to his actions. But war was in the air, and it was impossible to know how much longer it could be kept at bay.

Ernst stayed quiet. He showed up at the dairy in Neustettin where he had found work. Every morning, the farmers would bring their milk to that dairy. His assignment was to develop new varieties of cheese. On the job, he offered no cause for complaint, collected his pay, and tried not to make trouble.

But trouble found him. The Nazis he had crossed in Gross-Jestin extended their reach into Neustettin and again got Ernst fired from his job.

They were going to keep making his life difficult, and they weren't going to relent. And there was no way to make peace with them, no way to ask their forgiveness. If Ernst wanted to provide safety and stability for his family, he was going to have to find a way to make a living someplace where he was protected from the Nazis. So he did something unexpected.

He joined the army.

It was a great trick. By 1939, the Nazis had almost absolute power over the political and social spheres within Germany, and their influence was nearly inescapable. But Hitler's ambitions depended most of all on the army. He needed them, and that meant he needed to keep their chains of command happy. The military was the one body within German society that maintained some autonomy from the Nazis.

Ernst volunteered for the army, citing the boot camp training he had received when he was drafted into the military at the end of the Great War. He was promptly assigned to the local recruitment office, which meant that he was allowed to continue living at home. Each day he put on his military uniform, rode his bicycle across town, sat safely behind a desk for a few hours, and then biked back home. Many days he'd even pedal back to join his family for lunch. Everyone working in the office had mutually agreed not to make a practice of using the "Heil Hitler" salute that had become common throughout Germany. Miraculously, Ernst had managed to escape the threat of the Nazis and land a safe, stable, and sometimes even boring office job.

In the spring, the baby was born, and they named her Brunhild.

And finally, life in Neustettin began to settle into a relaxed routine. Food grew in the garden, the chickens laid healthy eggs, and Gertrud practiced her famous cooking, going so far as to prepare a rabbit or a duck on special occasions. Ernst took walks with his family in the woods, and they spent time together swimming in the lake, strolling through the park along the water's edge, and praying and studying the Bible. On Sundays, some of the town's other Baptists would gather at their home for a prayer meeting, and Ernst would preach. Daily he gave thanks, often thinking about how much he had to be thankful for.

It was—at least outwardly—a peaceful, happy time.

Then, on September 1, 1939, Hitler invaded Poland. Two days later, Britain and France responded by declaring war on Germany. World War II had begun.

CHAPTER 6

WLOCHY: 1939

LUDWIG JOB WAS an early riser.

He got up that day, the first of September 1939, a Friday, to head into the office well ahead of the official starting time. He liked to get there early, while it was still quiet. He enjoyed starting each workday privately, with a few calm rituals—sipping coffee and listening to the radio at his desk—before the rush of the day began in earnest, before people started coming and going through his lab and muddying his thoughts.

On his way out of his apartment, he took a quick peek at his three children, Eduard, Georg, and Elizabeth, all fast asleep, their tiny bodies delicate and still in their beds. He had played with his children the night before, and it made him smile to remember it. He loved them, of course, but he was also very impressed with them, these little dynamos—so active and tireless and filled with bottomless curiosity.

They take after their parents, he thought with a smile.

It was three days until his fifth wedding anniversary. He and Eveline were planning a little gathering in their apartment to celebrate with coffee and cake. He was looking forward to the chance to see his family and friends and to toast his happy marriage. As he stood in the doorway looking down on his little ones, he realized he'd gotten so wrapped up in thinking about the evening that he still didn't have any idea what to get Eveline for a present.

Typical Ludwig, he thought to himself, *always trying to solve the big problem but sometimes overlooking the immediate ones.* He was running out of time to decide.

At the entrance to the apartment building, Ludwig ran into his father-in-law, Julius Witt, who looked sternly at his watch. "You're a minute late," Julius teased. It was true: Ludwig did like to keep to his schedule, and today, for whatever reason, he was running uncharacteristically behind.

"I must be getting scatterbrained in my old age," he answered. They shared a smile and started their walk to the train.

The two men both still worked at the Philips plant—Julius was the plant's chief financial officer and Ludwig one of its leading research physicists—and their daily commute was also an important part of Ludwig's morning ritual.

"Have you heard from Bruno?" Ludwig asked.

Julius's son Bruno was an officer in the Polish army, and he'd been eagerly working his way through the ranks in hopes of becoming a career soldier. But the recent news coming out of Germany had started to unsettle the Witts. There were reports of border skirmishes between the Germans and the Poles, and the entire Polish army was on the brink of mobilizing for the possible outbreak of war.

Julius tried to put Ludwig at ease. "Everyone's skittish, of course. Hitler's saber rattling has seen to that. But war? It won't come to that. The Polish army has canceled its mobilization. Bruno's been ordered to stand down."

The two of them stood to disembark as the narrow-gauge train pulled into the station in the city, and then they made the short walk from there to the Philips plant. Julius had been with Philips since the start of its Warsaw operations in 1922 and had seen it become a buzzing place, with the number of its employees now well exceeding one thousand.

"I was wondering," Ludwig said before they parted ways. "Do you have any idea what I should get Eveline for an anniversary present?"

Julius laughed. "What do I know? I'm just her father."

Once in his office, Ludwig closed the door and flipped on the radio. It was a large tabletop radio that had been manufactured at this very plant. Ludwig knew it inside and out. He had been instrumental in developing the radio tubes that were now humming gently as they warmed up.

When the radio came to life, the voice of Adolf Hitler barked out of its speaker. Overnight, German troops had invaded Poland from the north, south, and west, and the Luftwaffe, the German air force, was soon to commence a bombing campaign on all major urban centers, including Warsaw.

The rumors had been true, after all. The German invasion had begun.

Ludwig tuned the dial to a local Polish news station. His full command of both German and Polish, and his fair knowledge of Russian, made it easy for him to flip between different broadcasts, and he wanted to learn what plans the Polish government was making to fight the German army.

Poland was in no way prepared to defend itself against a full-scale invasion by the German Wehrmacht. Ludwig knew it would be only a matter of time before the nation was occupied by German troops. The ease or difficulty of the coming days for the Polish people might just be a matter of how quickly or slowly their government surrendered.

Ludwig had been only a boy during the years of the Great War. He had no experience in how to protect his family from this sort of crisis.

On his way home in the evening, he heard a deep rumbling coming from the west. Surely it couldn't be the German military, this close already to Warsaw! Could they have advanced so far in one single day?

The evening news confirmed his suspicion. The Germans had advanced over a hundred miles in a single day, and the sounds Ludwig had heard were artillery and tanks in the war zone.

The noise got louder, closer, and more frequent over the coming days. The German troops, with the help of their very successful air force, advanced much more quickly than anybody would have thought possible. They penetrated deep into Poland, and the tanks of the 4th Panzerdivision had already reached positions just southeast of Warsaw. They held their line there, dug in, and didn't draw any closer—for now. The Polish military command of Warsaw had made it very clear that the city would be defended to the end. So before the Germans mounted a full siege of the city, they took a few days to make sure that the whole of Western Poland was firmly under their control.

The Jobs and Witts waited. It was a strange and emotionally confusing time for them. Though they were frightened of the coming invasion and had no way to guess how it might unsettle their lives, they also felt a discomfiting surge of pride. They were Polish, yes, but they were also German. They were part of what Hitler called the Volksdeutsche: true, ethnic Germans born and living in foreign countries as citizens of those nations yet considered by the Nazis to be as much a part of the Third Reich as the German nationals.

Ludwig couldn't guess what would happen to them once the Germans arrived in Warsaw. Would his work at Philips continue? Would their families be repatriated, given German citizenship, and drafted into the new German army? What would happen to Bruno Witt, his wife's brother, who was an officer in the Polish Army? Would he be offered special care because of his status as a Volksdeutscher? Or the opposite—would the Nazis consider him a traitor?

And what about their Polish friends and colleagues, the ones who weren't Volksdeutsche? What would happen to them?

He attempted to visualize how the Nazis might carry out the occupation of Poland in general and of Warsaw in particular. His mind drew a blank. Except for a few Polish newspaper articles and some German radio reports, he had nothing on which to base his thoughts. To be sure, a couple of years ago he had taken the train to the Philips headquarters in the Netherlands and for the first time in his life had gotten a glimpse of Germany, from the comfort of a German railroad car. It had not given him any revealing insights into the country under Nazi rule, although he had met at the borders officials in Nazi uniform who shouted the "Heil Hitler!" greeting and stamped his Polish passport. Ludwig's other interactions had been entirely with his Dutch superiors in Eindhoven.

What about Philips, the Dutch company that provided for the livelihoods of these two interwoven families, whose Warsaw plant was soon to come under German control? Philips designed and manufactured radios and other electronic devices that would certainly be of great value to the German war machine. What changes would that bring to the plant overall and to his research in particular? Would Ludwig now have to report to German superiors, and would he keep his position?

The days of September crawled on, everyone restless in anticipation of any news. Ludwig and Eveline went ahead with their anniversary dinner party, but it was a muted event, rather than the jubilant one they had planned.

For a gift, Ludwig went to their favorite baker and got Eveline a box of *chalwa*, the sesame bars she loved so much. The baker tied up the box in a ribbon and wished Ludwig and his wife a happy anniversary. On the way home, Ludwig also bought a bouquet of flowers.

He gave them to Eveline during the party. "Our marriage is good, right? Solid. I thought I might give you a good, solid gift to celebrate our anniversary—a wardrobe or a nice oaken table. I will still get you these things someday, I promise. But for now, with all this going on . . ." He looked out the window into the western evening sky, where the German artillery reportedly had dug in. "It is good to have things that are sweet and cheerful."

Eveline appreciated Ludwig's rare and sometimes awkward attempts at speaking poetically. "I already have something sweet," she said, kissing him on the cheek. "But I will never say no to chalwa!"

On Saturday, the ninth of September, Ludwig again rode the narrow-gauge rail to Warsaw on his way to the Philips plant. He was scheduled to work a half-day, but he also wanted to see if he could get any news about the impending attack.

As he took his short walk from the train station to the plant, he heard a series of loud cracks from the southeast—gunfire. The noise was immediately answered by louder, closer sounds coming from the well-positioned Polish defense force, soldiers who were dug into the hills.

The battle for Warsaw had begun.

German victory was practically certain, but it had also become clear that the Polish forces weren't going to give up the capital city without a fierce struggle. No one knew how long the fighting might drag on or how severely it would affect the people who lived there.

The Germans unleashed a relentless land and air bombardment of the city. The Jobs and Witts, in the outskirts, were mostly shielded from the bombing, but normal business life in the capital ground to a halt. There was nothing they could do but stay at home and pray for safety.

The battle raged on.

By now a number of nations, including England and France, had declared war on Germany, and the Polish defense strategy was to hold down a few strategic positions, including Warsaw, until help arrived. But that strategy fell apart on the seventeenth of September, when the country was unexpectedly invaded from the east by the Soviet Union. The Poles had no way of knowing when they'd planned their defense that Hitler and Stalin had already signed a nonaggression treaty that secretly divided the territory of Poland between the Nazis and the Soviets. The plan had been in place for a month or more, and Stalin had been amassing troops along the eastern border. Distracted by the attack in the west, no one had thought to look. The Poles were unable to fight a two-front war. As soon as news arrived of the Soviet invasion, Poland's leaders fled into exile in Romania.

Outside Warsaw, the German generals in charge of the attack knew their eventual victory was certain. They advised a conservative course: laying siege to the city and cutting off food and other supplies rather than launching an all-out attack that would risk lives on both sides. But Hitler rejected their recommendation and ordered massive bombing and shelling of the city. He wanted to pummel Warsaw into surrender.

The harsh battle continued for another ten days while the Jobs and Witts stayed in the shelter of their apartment in Wlochy, tuning the radio back and forth between German and Polish stations in search of news. It was the German radio station that first announced the surrender of Warsaw on September 27. Ludwig learned about it even before the Polish news station made it known to the population at large.

Though it was a defeat, he and his family breathed a sigh of great relief. The surrender meant an end to the Second Republic of Poland and to life as they had known it—but it also meant an end to the shelling, the bombs, and the destruction.

Ludwig watched from his office at the Philips plant as a long, victorious cavalcade of motorized German infantry arrived in the city of Warsaw and settled in.

The immediate problem had been solved, and now Ludwig put his mind to solving the bigger one: how to keep his family safe in the face of whatever was coming next.

CHAPTER 7

((•))

NEUSTETTIN: 1940–1941

IN APRIL 1940, German forces pushed north into Scandinavia. The following month, they headed west to invade France and the Low Countries. By mid-June, the German Blitzkrieg had overwhelmed the Allies and forced Denmark, Norway, Luxembourg, the Netherlands, and Belgium to surrender. The battle of France lasted barely over a month. Nazi forces rolled into Paris unopposed on June 14, and the French were forced to sign an armistice at Compiègne—the site of Germany's humiliating defeat in 1918 at the end of the First World War.

This Second Armistice at Compiègne turned the north and west of France over to the occupying Germans, including all its ports on the English Channel and the entire Atlantic coastline. The French government was deposed and replaced with a collaborationist regime, which was relocated from German-occupied Paris to Vichy, in the south of France.

In a few short months, Hitler had conquered most of northern Europe. While the Nazi-allied Italians began executing a campaign throughout the Mediterranean, Hitler turned his eye toward the foe he felt presented the biggest threat: Britain.

The Germans occupied positions around the European coast of the English Channel and the North Sea. In September 1940, the Luftwaffe began rattling London and other cities in England with relentless, sustained bombing raids that would continue for nearly a full year. This was known as the Blitz.

The British responded with frequent bombing raids of their own, hitting Berlin and other cities in Germany. On both sides of the Channel, people's lives were in upheaval. Almost everyone had family members drafted into one army or another. The ones who stayed home were enlisted to help in other ways. They rationed gas, food, and whatever supplies were needed for the war effort. Careers were repurposed according to the needs of the military. In industrial cities, families huddled at night in basements and in air raid shelters, living in fear of death from above. Daily life was changed dramatically.

But to an eight-year-old boy living in Pomerania in 1941, the war was a faraway thing.

Friedhelm wasn't just eight years old. He was eight and ten-twelfths years old. That was the same as eight and five-sixths years old. He knew this because he had already advanced to studying fractions during his two years at the Pestalozzi Elementary School in Neustettin. He was advancing so quickly that the school planned to graduate him a year early, after his third year. After that he was to attend the Fürstin Hedwig Oberschule, a well-known secondary school for selected students where Friedhelm's brother, Ernst-August, was already in attendance.

For the past two years, the Pestalozzi School had been teaching Friedhelm to read and write in the ornate German Gothic script, the same pointed script that had been in use throughout Germany for hundreds of years. It was the same script used by Gutenberg on his original printing press in the fifteenth century.

This year, though, the teachers handed Friedhelm new textbooks, each one emblazoned with a Nazi eagle and printed in a new Roman script. The books were filled with tiny, unreadable Roman letters, the same kind of letters they used in Britain and France. It wasn't fair.

Friedhelm was a good reader, but these new books were suddenly hard to read. It was like having to learn the alphabet all over again.

"Why can't we read the old way?" he asked his teacher. "The old way was better."

The teacher didn't have an easy answer. She didn't know how to explain to her eight- and nine-year-old students that these new textbooks were just one small part of a much larger plan the Third Reich had for Europe. The new German Empire was going to last for a thousand years, and from now on, people throughout the continent and the rest of the world would be reading their books in German.

The switch from the Gothic script to Roman was made in order to ease Europeans' transition from their various native tongues to the new universal language of German. Never mind the enormous cost of reprinting new textbooks for the entire country while financing the ever-growing Nazi war machine. Hitler's ambitions were so far-reaching that he fell under the spell of his own ideology: no expense was too great when it came to laying the groundwork for a thousand-year empire.

"You'll learn to read this way too," was the teacher's only answer. And sure enough, Friedhelm did learn the new way, and quickly.

Sometimes, though not too often, Friedhelm would see planes flying overhead—the fighters and bombers of the German Luftwaffe on their way to or from some faraway battle. He and his brother collected paper models of the planes: they built them with scissors, knives, and glue and painted them with numbers and crosses and insignia and vicious teeth, just like the real-life planes. Then they hung them from their bedroom ceiling and looked at the silhouettes of them as they fell asleep.

From the models, the boys learned to recognize and name many German aircraft by their shapes: the Heinkel He 111, the Messerschmitt Me 109, the Stuka Ju87 dive bomber, the Focke Wulf Fw190 fighter, and the Dornier D17*Fliegender Bleistift*—the Flying Pencil. The boys would shout out the names of the planes as soon as they spotted them in the sky and then wait until the planes flew overhead so they could see which ones they had guessed correctly. Ernst-August knew all the planes, and he could spot them from farther off than his friends. He was almost never wrong.

Friedhelm heard stories about the war on the Volksempfänger radio. There was always a report of some new victory. "*Sondermeldung!*" they always began, interrupting whatever other programming had been on the air. "*Sondermeldung!*" A special announcement.

Friedhelm and his friends sometimes reenacted these radio announcements while playing. "*Sondermeldung!*" one of them would stand up and announce. "The German Wehrmacht has seized El Agheila in Libya!"

"*Sondermeldung!* The Germans are victorious in Belgrade!"

"*Sondermeldung!* The Kriegsmarine declares a victory at sea in the Strait of Skagerrak!"

Friedhelm sometimes used the radio reports to learn geography: when battles were fought in the far-off towns in Africa or the Balkans or Scandinavia, he would find the names of the places in the index of his atlas, then find the spot on the map. He'd study the town and everything around it, and he'd think, *All of this, everything in this book, will soon be part of Germany.*

There were parades too, of troops and tanks moving through town. At the end of the parade, at the barracks in town, the troops drilled and marched and sometimes fired their guns for show, and then Friedhelm and his brother were allowed to go and look up close at the artillery. His brother convinced a soldier to let them climb onto one of the tanks, and Ernst-August peered down into the hatch and shouted "Hello!" to hear the echo of his voice bouncing around inside the metal while Friedhelm stared into the barrel of the giant turret.

But by and large, his life wasn't much affected by the war. He went swimming in the summer and skating in the winter. He went to school during the days and helped his mother with the garden and the chickens when he was home. On weekends, Friedhelm and Ernst-August would hike with their father through the woods. They had a car in their garage, a Ford Eifel, but they hadn't used it since the start of the war. The radio said "Every wheel is rolling toward victory!", meaning that everyone needed to conserve gasoline. To that end gas was strictly rationed, and only vehicles that were part of the war effort could obtain a *Bezugsschein*, a gasoline license. So they walked or rode bicycles; for very special trips, they took the train.

His dad was in the army, of course. Almost everyone's dad was in the army. Friedhelm watched each morning as Ernst buttoned up his gray-green wool field tunic and laced its dark green straps. The straps fascinated Friedhelm. The uniform was full of hooks and loops of fabric for hanging various pieces of equipment, and he would ask his father to explain which sorts of equipment went where. His father joked with him, telling him that this hook was for holding his lunch, and this hook was for chickens, and this one was so that he could strap himself into the kitchen table, and that one was for his bicycle seat. These last two hooks were so he could hold on to his two sons so that he would never lose them. It never occurred to Friedhelm that maybe his dad didn't know what the straps were actually for.

He knew that Ernst's job in the army wasn't like other soldiers' jobs. Most soldiers lived in barracks, and many of them lived far away from their families. Some of them never came back home. But his dad rode his bicycle to the recruitment office in the morning and came home again each night in time for dinner. It seemed to Friedhelm that his father's job in the army wasn't really much different than any of the other jobs he'd had, except that for this job he had to wear a special uniform.

One Sunday morning in the winter, he went for a walk with his dad. The two of them wandered over the frozen Lake Streitzig and into the forest. Fresh snow on the ground covered the trail markings, and they accidentally wandered into a nursery that was managed by a local forester to propagate young trees and that was strictly off limits. If they'd seen the signs they never would have entered the area, but with the snow they'd missed the trees completely and were horrified to be stepping on young plants that barely peeked through the white cover. As they quickly made their way toward the main path, the angry forester came out to meet them, and Friedhelm braced himself for a scolding from the man.

But as soon as the forester saw Ernst, dressed in his army uniform from the recruitment office, his demeanor changed completely. "So sorry to have disturbed your walk with your son, Herr Radandt."

Friedhelm saw plainly that this man was afraid of his father, but he did not understand why. On their way home he asked his dad about the incident: "Why was that forester afraid of you? Had he done something wrong?" His father did his best to explain: "No, he hadn't done anything wrong. It's because people are afraid that they will be called to become soldiers and then have to fight in the war. He was afraid that could happen to him." He didn't know how to make it clear to Friedhelm that the forester had begged to be allowed to stay in his job as a forester and not be drafted into the military. In the uncertain time of war, Ernst Radandt found himself in a position of some influence.

Ernst-August, two years older than Friedhelm, was already a member of the Deutsches Jungvolk, the Nazi organization for boys. On Saturdays and Wednesdays, Ernst-August's teachers didn't assign him any homework. Instead, he was allowed to put on a uniform with the lightning-shaped *Sieg* symbol sewn onto the sleeve and go off with the other boys to marching drills. These drills involved singing marching songs, periods of instruction and testing, and shooting at targets with rifles. Sometimes they would hike and go camping.

Friedhelm wanted to go too, but he wasn't allowed, and he wouldn't be allowed until he turned ten. Ernst-August showed him some of what he learned with the Jungvolk. He taught him first aid and how to tie knots and put up a tent. But he wouldn't let Friedhelm try on his uniform.

"You'll get your own uniform," he said, "when you're ten."

Friedhelm wasn't going to turn ten for a long time, not until October 23, 1942. That was more than a year away. He could hardly wait.

One fine day in June 1941, he walked with his brother through Neustettin. At the train station, he saw the strangest thing: though it was summer, people were lined up, and all of them were holding skis. When they got to the front of the line, they handed the skis and other winter gear to some army men, who loaded them onto a train car.

"I don't understand," Friedhelm said to his brother. "Why does the army need skis? Where are they going?"

Ernst-August was only eleven years old, but he seemed to have an innate understanding of things. Or maybe he'd simply overheard conversations during his Jungvolk meetings that weren't meant for a young boy's ears. But he knew instantly what the skis were for.

"The army needs skis," he explained to his little brother, "because they're going to Russia."

The treaty of nonaggression that had been signed by the Germans and the Russians in 1939 had kept the war out of Pomerania and eastern Germany. But a mere week after France surrendered, Hitler on June 22, 1941 would break his pact with Stalin and invade the Soviet Union. It would become the largest and deadliest invasion in the history of warfare.

CHAPTER 8

POLAND: 1940–1941

"HAVE YOU HEARD from Bruno?"

In the months that followed the German invasion of Poland, there were many changes in the lives of Ludwig Job and the Witt family, but none was as pressing as their desire to track down Eveline's brother and Julius Witt's son, Bruno.

Bruno had fought with the Polish army against the German invaders right up until the army surrendered, and since then they'd heard nothing. They didn't know if he was wounded or killed, or if he had been taken prisoner. If Bruno were a prisoner, they didn't know whether his German ethnicity would mean more favorable treatment by the German soldiers . . . or harsher treatment. Would he be considered a traitor because he had fought on the side of the Poles? Would they want to punish him in order to set an example for the others?

Bruno's wife, Tatiana, and his young son, Victor, lived in the apartment building in Wlochy with the rest of the family. Tatiana was Russian by birth, tall and stunningly beautiful. Everyone wanted to find information to ease their worry. It would have been simple enough for the family to walk to the German army's headquarters in Warsaw and find out if they had lists of Polish officers who had been taken prisoner.

But they didn't want to alert the German authorities to Bruno's ethnicity until they had a clearer idea whether this would make things better for him or worse.

So they made the harder choice and did nothing. They waited for news and quietly asked any of their friends who might have information, "Have you heard from Bruno?"

The occupying army had indeed identified the Witts and Jobs as Volksdeutsche, ethnic Germans. As such, the family was enlisted to house German soldiers in their apartment building. The Witts turned the ground floor of the building over to the soldiers, and over the course of time they became acquainted with them. But this relationship still didn't lead to any new information about their son and brother, because no one in the family dared to bring up the topic.

In many other ways, life in Warsaw quickly resumed its normal pace, at least on the surface. The German government assessed Ludwig Job's skills and experience and decided he would do the most good for the war effort if he stayed in his position at the Philips plant, researching and developing superior radio tubes. Radio technologies were highly valued by the military for its communication needs, and therefore so was Ludwig Job. The Germans armed him with a revolver to help keep him safe, trained him in its use, and then sent him back to work.

Once again, Ludwig returned to his old rituals, getting up early each morning for work, riding the commuter train from Wlochy, then walking the short distance from the train station to the Philips plant.

Now, though, he had to do it without his father-in-law. Julius Witt and his wife had decided shortly after the start of the German occupation to move out of the apartment in suburban Wlochy and into their home within the Warsaw city limits, in the heart of the German neighborhood. They said it was to help keep the house safe during these strange, unsettled times, but the fact was that it wasn't just safer for the house. Since the invasion, the ethnic Germans in Warsaw had quickly discovered that it was safer for them, too, if they stayed together. Though they'd lived side by side with the Poles for generations, the occupation had created tension between the two ethnic groups, which was exacerbated by the Germans' preferential treatment of the Volksdeutsche and their harsh treatment of the Poles.

It took a few months before the German occupation forces had the city under full control and before Ludwig's children, early in 1940, started up again at their German preschool. A year later, in the spring of 1941, the school was mounting a play, one of the Grimm Brothers' fairy tales, and four-year-old Elizabeth was cast in the role of *Sleeping Beauty*. She was excited to play the role of a princess, and she rehearsed her scenes at home with her family, reenacting over and over the part of the play in which she pricked her finger on the spindle and fell into a deep, death-like sleep.

"Oh, what would make her waken?" Eveline read from the play script, running the lines to help Elizabeth practice.

Ludwig watched his little girl lying on the parlor floor, so beautiful and sweet-faced and still, and he became suddenly upset. For a moment, he believed the illusion. He imagined that his little Elizabeth couldn't be woken, that some dark magic had stricken his daughter down right there in their home and nothing he could do would wake her. What evil would do this to a little girl, to an innocent? What would make her awake? Love for his daughter poured out of his heart, and he realized he would do anything to protect her and keep her safe. Anything.

She poked her head up and peeked out through her half-closed eyes. "Daddy!" He had missed his cue.

"Love," he read from the script. "If a man of pure heart were to love her, that would bring her back to life."

He kissed his little girl on the forehead, but then he had to leave the room.

Ludwig learned at work that the German army had taken the Netherlands and that the Eindhoven headquarters of the Philips corporation was now under German control. It amazed him to realize that despite the violent change roiling Europe, his own life was continuing nearly as it had been before the start of the war. His rituals were nearly unaltered. He got up early. He rode the train. He worked in his lab. He returned home to his family.

Each day on his commute he looked out the window of his railcar and could see the changes slowly altering Warsaw. He saw streetcars that offered seats only to Volksdeutsche like himself. He saw soldiers corralling native Poles, whom the Nazis considered *Untermensch*, inferior people, and conscripting them into forced labor. He saw the construction of the Warsaw Ghetto.

But it all seemed very far away. His own life was unchanged.

He got up early. He rode the train. He worked in his lab. He returned home to his family.

He would do anything to keep them safe.

"We've heard from Bruno!" Julius bounded into Ludwig's lab at work with a letter in his hand.

His brother-in-law had been captured during the German invasion and assigned to a prisoner of war camp, along with fellow officers in the Polish army. As soon as the prisoners were allowed to write to their families, Bruno had sent a letter to his parents to let everyone know that he was alive.

Though they didn't know it until later, Bruno had given a lot of thought to the letter, and how to write it. He was certain his captors would read it. He had gone to great trouble while in captivity to hide his ethnic origin from the Germans; he still didn't know how they would receive the news that he, an ethnic German, had sided against them during the invasion. He wanted to be sure that the letter he wrote to his family would not reveal anything new to the Germans, so he wrote it in Polish. The soldiers in the prisoner of war camp would still be able to understand its contents, but at least they wouldn't wonder about this Polish officer who communicated with his family in the German tongue.

Of course Bruno also wanted to send a letter to his wife. But Tatiana's father had been a general in the Russian army before the Bolshevik Revolution and had fled to Poland when the Communists came to power. He and his family were all considered enemies of the Soviet Union. Bruno was unsure how this relationship would be perceived by the Germans at the camp, who were still allies of Russia, and he wanted to avoid writing anything that might draw unwanted attention to himself. He sent one carefully worded letter to his parents and asked them to relay the news to Tatiana and to the rest of the family.

His parents were so excited to hear from him that they immediately wrote a letter back to him—in German. All of Bruno's efforts at hiding his heritage were for nothing. As soon as the camp received the reply letter, the German colonel in charge of the camp had Bruno escorted to a locked room and began to interrogate him about his background.

"Are you German?" the colonel asked him in Polish.

Bruno knew nothing of the letter that his parents had sent to the camp and didn't know what the colonel knew. He chose his words carefully. "I'm Polish," he said. "I was born in Poland."

"Your parents—they are German?"

Bruno had never been interrogated before. He used what he had learned in his officer training to try to control his fear, but still he felt his palms sweating and his heart racing. "My parents are also Polish."

The colonel nodded. "Yet they write in German." He put the letter down on the table in front of Bruno. All was lost. The secret was out.

The colonel dropped the pretense of speaking Polish and switched to German. "Listen to me. Things could get very bad for you, Bruno Witt—things could get ghastly—if you do not tell me the truth. I'll ask you once again. Are you German?"

Bruno didn't know what to expect from the Nazis, but he knew there was no point in trying to keep his heritage a secret any longer. "Yes," he confessed. "I am German."

"Very good," the colonel answered and stood up. "I just needed you to say it. You will be returned to your family. You and all of the Volksdeutsche in Poland are very important to us, to the Reich."

And like that, Bruno's time in captivity was over. Within days, Bruno was released. He said good-bye to his comrades in the camp and wished them luck. Then he went home, where he was welcomed by his wife and his son, Victor, and the rest of the relieved Witt family.

Soon after, the Germans in charge of the prisoner of war camp delivered the remaining Polish officers to the Soviets in accordance with an agreement the two nations had in place regarding the division of spoils in Poland. Once the prisoners—Bruno's former comrades—arrived at the Soviet camp in Katyn, they were summarily executed. Bruno had escaped certain death.

In Poland, all of the Volksdeutsche were required to submit an *Ahnenpass*, a "passport" that proved German ancestry. Ludwig Job presented his papers on behalf of himself and his family. The form asked for information about his wife, Eveline, his parents, and his grandparents on both his mother's and his father's side. There was no room on the form for Eveline's ancestry. Apparently, if Ludwig could show German surnames and German Christian names as far back as his grandparents, that was sufficient.

In time, he and his family were granted new citizenship papers.

"We are German now," he told them with a twinkle in his eyes.

It was hard to tell whether he was pleased about their new status or whether he was somewhat apprehensive about this action that declared them to be German nationals. The longer the occupation lasted, the more visible and frightening grew the rift that separated the Polish population from the Volksdeutsche in their midst. The Jobs had always thought of themselves as part of a culturally German minority in Poland. But these new citizenship papers identified them as foreigners in the land they called home, while aligning them more closely with the German occupation force. Ludwig dealt daily with Polish colleagues and employees at work. He heard their complaints and felt for them. But they and he needed the job, and they both knew that under German control, Philips in Warsaw was manufacturing radio tubes that benefited the war effort, something he preferred not to think about.

Ludwig and his family moved out of the apartment in Wlochy and into a house in the German district of Warsaw. They were closer to the Philips plant and just a few blocks from Eveline's parents. And it was safer for them there. The Polish resistance was growing. The nationalistic pride and identity of the Polish people loomed larger in their hearts and minds as they saw their homeland completely wiped off Germany's newly produced maps of central Europe.

And then the Germans invaded the Soviet Union and opened up the Eastern Front. War had come back to Poland.

CHAPTER 9

NEUSTETTIN: 1942–1943

THE STRANGE LADY had four suitcases and a baby, and she was moving them all into Friedhelm's house. His father was already carrying the lady's heaviest luggage, a steamer trunk, up the stairs. In the parlor, Gisela cooed over the baby while Gertrud greeted the lady like an old friend, even though Friedhelm was certain that none of them had ever met her before today.

She was from another part of Germany, the city of Bochum in the Ruhr district, all the way across the country—some five hundred miles to the west. Even her accent sounded strange to Friedhelm's ears. She had traveled to Neustettin by train with her suitcases and her baby.

Friedhelm's grandfather, August Rattunde, was in from Kolberg for the day, to greet the lady and to make her feel welcome—or so he said. But he was also here to keep Friedhelm occupied while Ernst and Gertrud helped their new guest get settled in.

The two of them stood across the yard, under the trees. Friedhelm pretended to feed the chickens while he watched this newcomer stepping out onto the balcony and taking in her new surroundings. "Where is her husband? Why isn't he helping with the suitcases?"

"Her husband is an officer in the army. He's stationed in the barracks here in Neustettin. He'll come visit us later tonight."

"How long is she staying here?"

"I don't know the answer to that question," his grandfather told him. "Even she doesn't know the answer to that question."

The woman's home in the Ruhr had come under heavy Allied bombing that had killed thousands of people and destroyed more than half the region's homes. German authorities evacuated many citizens of the Ruhr and relocated them to safer districts in Germany, and that was how this woman and her baby found their way to Pomerania. All this August Rattunde told Friedhelm. "She'll stay until it's safe for her to go home."

Friedhelm liked his grandfather. He liked that his grandfather always told him the truth, even when the truth was frightening. Even when the truth was that he didn't know the answer.

He watched as his dad pulled a second heavy trunk up the stairs. "Why did the lady bring so many things?"

His grandfather looked at him with his big, kind eyes. "Imagine, Friedhelm, what it must be like for this woman. Imagine having to leave your own home suddenly, without warning. Planes are flying overhead, dropping bombs everywhere. Your neighborhood is on fire. The baby is crying. You don't know if you will ever be able to return to your house. Soldiers come and tell you that you must go on a train to a town where you know no one, and you must start your life over again, with nothing but the things you can fit into your luggage. If that happened to me, I would bring as many things as I could. I would fill up as many suitcases as I could carry. Wouldn't you?"

Friedhelm nodded. "I guess."

"Now let's go say hello to the woman and help your father with that luggage."

They helped the woman unpack her things in a room that had been used by Friedhelm's grandmother, and then they left her some privacy.

When she came out of the room, she'd changed out of the clothes she'd been wearing and into a fresh dress. She was somewhat large, and with her strikingly black hair, looked very young. Her husband was coming over at dinnertime, and Friedhelm's mother and sister were cooking up a duck to celebrate. They prepared the duck in the classic Pomeranian way his mother had learned when she was young. The Radandts impressed their new guests with both their cooking and their hospitality.

The couple were Baptists, like the Radandts. When they learned that Grandfather August was a lay preacher, they asked him to lead them in a prayer before dinner.

"I'll say a few words, if you like," Grandfather said. "But I don't want the duck to get cold, so I promise not to take too long." He winked at them and then reached into his coat for his well-thumbed Bible, opened it to the gospel of Luke, and cleared his throat.

"I'm sure everyone at this table knows the story of the Good Samaritan, but tonight, please let me refresh your memory. Once there was a traveler going from Jerusalem to Jericho, and he fell upon a gang of robbers. The man was beaten, stripped of his possessions, and left for dead by the side of the road. A priest came upon this man, and though his suffering was apparent for all to see, the priest did nothing to help the man—just crossed to the other side of the road and walked on. Later, another man, a Levite, did the same: he saw the unfortunate traveler in need of help, but passed him by.

"Finally, a Samaritan came—and in these times, no one thought very kindly of Samaritans—but this Samaritan stopped for the traveler. He helped him up, nursed his wounds, and took him to an inn. And when the traveler recovered, the Samaritan didn't just let him continue on his journey, but made sure he would have some money too, to ease his travels.

"Jesus told his disciples that 'He who loves his neighbor as himself does the will of God.' So today we take in this family, and we will treat you as our own."

"Amen," said the family.

But though the duck was getting cold, Grandfather was not yet finished. "Dear God," he continued, "we are not here today to ask your gratitude for the kindness we hope to offer to this family in need. Rather, we are here to express our gratitude to you that we have so much to share. We are here to give thanks to you for guiding this family to us during their time of need, that we may help one another on our journey to you. Today we are privileged to be the Good Samaritans, and we will offer refuge to this family the best we can, like neighbors—because we can never know, in our own lives, when we will be the host or when we will be the unfortunate traveler in need of kindness; when we will be able to offer mercy to others or when we will need to ask it from them. Amen."

"Amen," everyone said, and then they ate the scrumptious duck, which was still crispy and warm and perfect.

At night, everyone in town covered up their windows so no light would leak out. Though no bombs had yet fallen in Neustettin, they were under orders to be cautious. Light spilling from windows made easy targets for bombers that flew overhead in the nighttime.

Lying in bed, Friedhelm heard the far-off churn of a plane engine somewhere above them. "Stuka," Friedhelm said to his brother, trying to guess at the type of plane.

"It's not a Stuka," Ernst-August answered, half-asleep.

"If you're so sure, go check."

His brother rolled out of bed and pulled back a curtain from the bedroom window. The night was dark, and the plane was too far away for him to see, but still he insisted.

"It's not a Stuka," he whispered back through the darkness. "It's a Peshka. It's VVS. It's Russian."

"A Russian plane? Here?"

"It's just flying past."

They listened as the sound of the plane grew fainter, and Friedhelm breathed a little easier. "Ernst-August," he asked. "How far is it from Neustettin to Russia?"

"It's far. Very far."

"But the Russian plane, the Peshka—it can fly very far, right?"

For a while, Ernst-August didn't answer. "The Peshka is probably lost. The Luftwaffe will shoot it down before it ever makes it back home."

They lay back down in their beds, but Friedhelm couldn't fall asleep. He held his breath to keep quiet, trying to hear the sounds of the faraway plane. He couldn't tell if his brother had drifted off to sleep. "Ernst-August? Will the Russians bomb Neustettin?"

But he got no answer—just Ernst-August's easy breathing in the quiet night.

The Russians were getting closer. There was no news of it on the radio, but there were more and more signs of it in town: trains packed full of young soldiers heading east, trains packed with wounded soldiers heading west. More and more planes in the sky, and not all of them German planes.

Hitler had assumed the German invasion of the Soviet Union, which started in June of 1941, would take several months to complete. He planned to utterly defeat an untrained and underprepared Red Army at Leningrad and Smolensk and then roll into Moscow by the end of 1941, victorious and unopposed, as quickly and easily as he had conquered Paris in the summer of 1940.

But the Russians had proved better trained, better equipped, and far, far more numerous than Hitler had imagined. Instead of achieving a crushing victory at Leningrad, the German Wehrmacht found itself in the midst of a bloody, years-long siege with no end in sight. South of Leningrad, the Germans were repelled from Moscow with heavy casualties on both sides.

The two sides fought long, bitter battles across an 1,800-mile front, and after a year of deadly stalemates, the Germans launched a second large-scale attack on Moscow.

Again, the Soviets fought them off. And again, the harsh winter settled in and forced the Germans to retreat, committing them to another long year of fighting in the no-man's land of the Ukraine.

By the spring of 1943, the skis that the German people had several years earlier shipped to the Eastern Front to assist the army with their invasion of Russia were returned. A truckload made its way to Neustettin and was dumped unceremoniously in a heap at the train station. When Ernst-August and Friedhelm discovered the pile of skis, which were free for the taking, they tried on different pairs and picked out their favorites. They'd never had skis before, and they were eager to try them out during the coming winter. They didn't wonder why the army had returned the skis, why they were no longer needed for the war effort.

But the answer was clear enough. The German generals knew there would be no third opportunity for them to invade Moscow. Now it was all the Wehrmacht could do to hold the line in the Ukraine and keep the Soviets from advancing further west.

The Eastern Front was collapsing. The Russians were getting closer. And there was little anyone could do to stop them.

CHAPTER 10

WARSAW: 1942–1943

LUDWIG JOB CLOSED the sliding door to his train compartment, collapsed into his seat, and relaxed for the first time in days. He loosened his tie and gazed out the window at the people passing through the Hamburg Hauptbahnhof. It was a typical assortment of hurried business travelers like himself and soldiers, some of them banded together, some saying good-bye to loved ones, some sitting alone, clutching duffel bags and staring off into space, their thoughts hidden behind their opaque expressions.

He also saw the *Schutzstaffel*, the "SS," wearing their Nazi uniforms and patrolling the station, checking travelers' papers before they boarded their trains.

Ludwig loved his trips to Hamburg, but he was glad to be going home. He had been called to the city in order to present his latest research to his higher-ups at Philips. Back at the Warsaw plant, his team had come up with a new idea for producing radio tubes with greater noise reduction than any that Philips currently manufactured. They had gone as far as developing some prototypes for demonstration purposes, but they couldn't go into production until they'd earned the approval of the administrators. This trip was Ludwig's chance to impress them, to present the prototypes and to convince Philips to adopt his innovation.

Ever since the German invasion of the Netherlands, the Philips plant in Hamburg had become the *de facto* center of the continental European operations for the company. In addition to its impressive plant in Hamburg-Lokstedt, Philips also maintained an imposing building of administrative offices right in downtown Hamburg, just a few blocks from Alster Lake and from the Hotel Atlantik where Ludwig stayed during his visits.

On the whole, Ludwig was taken in by Hamburg. He admired the city's architecture and found the place stimulating. And he was more than impressed with Philips' Hamburg laboratories and production facilities. The researchers in Hamburg treated Ludwig as one of their own—a valued and valuable member of their team. "Ludwig, how have you been?" they greeted him when he arrived. "How is your little daughter?" They always demanded to see photos of his little girl, Elizabeth.

"She's five now," he would say. "Can you believe it?"

His presentation to the team had gone very well. As always, they were impressed with his work. "You should come out here," the team leader had told him, "as soon as the Warsaw plant closes."

Ludwig thanked the man and nodded and shook his hand. He was indeed very interested in joining the team in Hamburg whenever the war came to an end. But why had the man been so convinced that the Warsaw plant would be closing?

Ludwig thought back on this conversation and others as his train pulled out of the Hauptbahnhof. He could see from the outside of the station that the building had taken some damage from the Allied bombs. Its east side was partially crumbled and fenced off, and one of its clock towers had been completely destroyed.

Bombing damage was apparent throughout the city. The air raids were clearly taking a toll, though Ludwig had so far been lucky enough not to experience any of them firsthand. He thought about them plenty.

While in the city, he was careful always to make a mental note of the bomb shelters he saw—their locations and which ones were closest to him at any given time, and how he would get to one if the air raid sirens were to go off.

He knew that a train car was one of the worst places to be during a bombing raid, because there is no way to hide a train and no way for the passengers to run to safety. And because the trains were also used to transport troops and supplies for the Wehrmacht, the Allies considered them legitimate strategic targets.

He tried to put all of this out of his mind and to think about work. He closed his eyes while the train hurtled through the German countryside. By the time he opened them again, the train was already at Schwarzenbek, exactly on schedule. Miraculously, the rail service seemed barely altered by the war.

Say what you will about the Germans, Ludwig thought, *but they do know how to run a train*. During war as well as during peace, the Deutsche Reichsbahn would get you to your destination on time.

"How is your little daughter?" they had asked him. He never told them what he was really thinking. "She's upset," he wanted to say. "Elizabeth is upset by this war."

Several months before Ludwig had taken this trip, he and Eveline had been walking through the city of Warsaw with Elizabeth. It was a beautiful, warm Sunday, and they took a meandering walk home from church, trying to enjoy every last bit of sunshine before the day ran out. So it was that they accidentally came upon the fence surrounding the Warsaw Ghetto.

There, just at the moment they'd arrived, they saw two young children, apparently a brother and sister, trying to climb out from underneath the barbed wire fence. The boy, a little older, managed to scamper through a gap, though the wire scraped at his arms and face. But the little girl—Elizabeth's age, maybe, or just a year or so younger—was too slow. The soldiers who guarded the fence caught her before she made it out.

They kicked her back under the fence with their boots while guards in the ghetto grabbed her ankles and dragged her back inside. Her brother, who from across the street had been beckoning his sister feverishly with his right hand to follow him, didn't know what to do. He didn't know how to help her. What *could* he do? So he watched from the shadows, paralyzed, as those soldiers hit his sister and carried her away. Then the boy turned and ran up the ascending street and disappeared from sight. Left standing behind the barbed wire was a small group of haggard figures in drab black and grey coats and hats, with their eyes to the ground. They showed no emotion. Had they not noticed the cruel treatment of the girl?

Elizabeth saw all of this. Ludwig and Eveline held her hand tightly and tried to rush past to the next street. Ludwig tried to put his body between his daughter and that terrible ghetto, to keep her from seeing inside. But nothing could erase what she had seen.

Once they were safely past, he wanted to say something to Elizabeth, to explain what had happened, to comfort her—but what could he possibly say? How could he possibly put the child's mind at ease after that?

He couldn't even put his own mind at ease.

Ludwig's sister Olga had recently told him a dreadful story from her farm in rural Poland. She'd been working in the fields on a very hot summer day when a train rattled by. It was one of those transports bound for nearby Treblinka, a cattle car loaded terribly full with people—Jewish people. The train came to a stop right by the field—it must have been waiting for another train to clear the track—and the people began reaching through the slats of the cattle car, calling out and begging for a drink of water. Olga's neighbor had a can of water handy, and she offered it to the people in the car. But the SS who were guarding the train climbed down off the car and knocked the can out of the woman's hands.

"If you do that again," the man had told her, "you go with them."

Everyone knew what was happening in Treblinka. Everyone

knew but didn't know how to talk about it. Olga told Ludwig, "Some days, we can see the smoke rising from that camp. It has the smell of burned flesh."

Ludwig shuddered to imagine it. Could it be that the Jewish people on those cattle cars near Olga's farm had come from this ghetto in his hometown of Warsaw? And could it be that once this transport delivered its cargo to Treblinka, these human beings would be burned to death? It was a thought he wanted to squash and push back into the taciturn regions of his mind. He simply couldn't bring himself to talk about what they had witnessed, not to his wife, not to his sister, not to anyone.

The train was speeding along, and Ludwig did not want to think further about the matter.

Instead, he tried to think of radio tubes, coils of wire, melting solder, the warm hum of electricity, and all the work that awaited him once he returned home.

Was Philips really planning to close the plant in Warsaw? What would become of his family if they did? He wanted to talk to his father-in-law. Julius had recently retired and moved out of Warsaw entirely, into the city of Lodz, inside the newly designated German district called the Warthegau. But he still had a lot of friends at Philips. If there were a plan afoot to close the plant, Julius would know about it.

"Papers?" Two uniformed Nazis pushed their way into Ludwig's compartment, asking to see his travel permit. It was unusual for any German man of Ludwig's age to be traveling without a military uniform, and these men were undoubtedly checking to see if Ludwig might be a deserter.

"My papers are in my briefcase. One moment." His signed papers were all in order, but still the men made him nervous. He wasn't doing anything wrong, but it would be too easy for a misunderstanding to get out of hand. Ludwig's hands sweated as he fumbled with the lock on his briefcase, and it took him three tries to open it.

"Here you are," he said, handing the papers over. He saw the tremor in his hand as he offered the papers to the men, but he couldn't tell if they noticed.

The Nazis scrutinized Ludwig's paperwork and then wished him a good day. Ludwig listened to their footsteps as they made their way through the compartment coach and on to the next railcar.

Win or lose, he caught himself thinking. *Either way I don't care, as long as the war is over soon*. He knew it was a traitorous thought and that he would never dare to speak it out loud.

The train made its way steadily east, and its rhythmic rocking on the tracks lulled Ludwig into a deep, unplanned sleep. Before he knew it, he was back home.

"Daddy!" His little Elizabeth was waiting for him at the train station with Eveline. The two wore light coats that kept them warm in the cool evening air. They had stepped onto the platform just a few minutes before the train's scheduled arrival and had watched Ludwig get off the first-class railroad car.

He scooped Elizabeth up in his arms. "It's awfully late for a young girl to be awake!"

"She insisted," Eveline explained. "She was so excited to see you, I couldn't get her to sleep."

Their walk home was quiet except for Elizabeth's storytelling; she wanted to catch her father up on everything that had been going on in her school. Ludwig half-listened to her while he looked around the empty Warsaw streets. It was past curfew, but the curfew didn't apply to the Germans, only to the Poles. There were many new rules and regulations that applied only to the Poles. Ludwig knew them well on account of the number of Polish coworkers he had. For instance, Polish citizens weren't allowed to own radios, under penalty of death—a regulation against which Philips had argued and even gotten a temporary reprieve, at least for its employees. How could they be expected to work on radios if they weren't allowed to own radios? The company won that point and its employees were allowed to purchase radios as long as they promised not to listen to foreign radio stations and not to allow other Polish citizens to join them while they listened to any radio programs at all.

For all the supposed efficiency of the Nazis, Ludwig thought, they had more than their share of ridiculous regulations.

Ludwig considered himself to be a friend of the Polish people. He worked with Poles every day, and he did what he could to advocate on their behalf. He heard stories from them about their plight under the Nazi occupation. He also heard rumors about the growing Polish resistance, and he heard too that some of its members were employed by Philips, maybe even on Ludwig's own research team. These undercover resistance fighters engaged in sabotage of some of the electronic communication equipment designed for use by the German navy. For Ludwig and other members of the management team, this was a scary development.

Had he known how deeply the resistance was at work in Philips, he would not have slept at night. One of the top young resistance fighters in Warsaw, Edmund Baranowski, worked for Philips while at the same time completing his advanced secondary education in an underground school run by the resistance movement. Baranowski knew the inner workings of the plant, including its manufacturing procedures and its production schedules. He also knew the staff—who they were, what projects they were assigned to, and how important each of these projects was to the German war effort. With Baranowski's help, the Polish resistance compiled a list of Philips employees who were considered instrumental to the Nazis and sentenced everyone on that list to death.

One of the names on that list was the researcher in charge of supplying the German government with radio tubes vital to its military and propaganda efforts—Ludwig Job.

CHAPTER 11

NEUSTETTIN: 1943–1944

JUST OVER THIRTY PEOPLE had squeezed into the Radandts' house at 34 Bugenhagenstrasse, among them a number of young people, and they were all singing.

The German Baptist community of Neustettin had been growing, especially since the arrival of the refugee families from Bochum. But the closest Baptist church to Neustettin was in Belgard, a one-hour trip by train. On special occasions, like Easter, the Radandts and several of the other Baptists from town would trek to Belgard and join the larger community for their celebration of the holiday. Friedhelm's sister Gisela had been baptized at the church in Belgard.

But most Sundays, the Radandts offered their friends another option: they opened their doors for prayer meetings in their own home.

They had a bit of a chair problem. In the beginning, when the meetings were small, Friedhelm and his brother would wake on Sundays to help their parents rearrange their living room furniture to accommodate the extra guests. Before long, they were adding chairs from their dining room, and then from their kitchen. Lately more people were attending their house church each Sunday than they had chairs for. Some of their guests had taken to leaning against the wall or even sitting on the floor to save available seats for their elders and for the women with babies.

But everyone always managed to fit inside.

The prayer meetings were an important part of the practice of their faith: a chance to ruminate on passages from the Bible, to reflect on them and discuss them with other members of the community. Not everyone agreed on how all the passages should be interpreted, but that was exactly the point. The discussion allowed them to see other points of view and perhaps, through reflection, even come to different and maybe more profound understandings.

No matter how heated the Sunday discussions got, the house church was joyous too, thanks in no small part to the singing. There was always singing. Everyone loved the hymns. Some of the ladies in the church prepared a bundle of hand-typed hymnals and handed them out every Sunday. When the house was full of people, the chorus of their voices echoed off the wood floors and carried, Friedhelm imagined, at least as far as Lake Streitzig . . . if not all the way to Berlin.

After the prayers and singing ended, people would linger in the living room and in the kitchen, eating snacks and telling stories and celebrating a very real and very precious community—practically a family. For these Christian friends, coming together for prayer and worship offered them the opportunity to escape for a short time the harsh reality of a devastating war and of the ever more encroaching Nazi ideology. The news of the losing battle in Russia made them wonder whether Germany was on the right track. But it seemed wiser not to talk about it, especially not about instances of alleged euthanasia within Germany or of policies that had exiled Jews to work camps. More recently, even slight criticism of the Nazi party and its programs or failure to fly the flag with the swastika on Hitler's birthday led to harsh reprisals. Citizens had simply disappeared with no reasons given.

Almost all of the worshippers in the living room of the Radandts that Sunday worried about family members fighting in the war. The pastors of the nearest Baptist churches, the one in Belgard and the one in Kolberg, had been drafted as well and shipped to the front line. Prayers were offered for these soldiers, but thoughts about the Führer were kept to oneself.

Friedhelm's father was proud of the fact that no matter how large the group grew, he would never turn anyone away. "There is always room for another in this house, no matter how many people come knocking at the door."

Then, on this particular Sunday, the Nazis knocked on the door.

"*Shhh, shhh!* Everyone, please be quiet."

A hush came quickly over the house church, as whispers spread about the uninvited guests.

"Perhaps if we ignore them, they'll just go away."

But the two men standing on the front porch of 34 Bugenhagenstrasse, neatly dressed in their Nazi uniforms, weren't so easily dissuaded. They rapped hard on the door a second time.

Though the Baptists were not part of the official Protestant state church of Germany—this role belonged to the Evangelische Kirche, which was predominantly Lutheran—there was nothing untoward about practicing the Baptist faith. Generations earlier, Baptists had been considered a dissident religion by the German state and faced persecution by the Lutherans and the government. But now the members of the Baptist church lived peacefully alongside their Lutheran brethren. Baptists were a minority, to be sure, and affiliation with the Baptist church in the otherwise Lutheran Germany led to some inconveniences and occasional misunderstandings. But it was not illegal.

Ernst didn't know what the Nazis wanted, but he didn't want trouble. He still had not forgotten the struggles he'd had with the Nazi Party a few years earlier, when he had been forced out of his job in Gross-Jestin—and he doubted that the Nazis had forgotten the incident, either. As far as he was concerned, no visit from the Nazis was a good visit. But the timing this afternoon was particularly unfortunate.

Now that the German war effort had stalled in Russia and in Africa, a new fear was creeping through the homeland. For the first time, people had begun to wonder, *What will happen if the Nazis lose the war*? Whispers of discontent were spreading through Pomerania: maybe Hitler was not the best leader for Germany after all.

And the Nazis did everything in their power to quiet those whispers.

Ernst knew these Nazi officials would not look kindly on any meeting—let alone so large a meeting—in the private home of someone who had already stood in opposition to their party.

He was not doing anything wrong, he reminded himself as he slid closed the two pocket doors to the living room. He was amazed at his friends in the prayer group. They had been loud and jubilant only moments earlier, and now they sat so still and silent behind those pocket doors that the house seemed completely empty.

"Good afternoon," he said to the Nazis as he unlocked the front door. "Sorry to keep you waiting."

"Good afternoon, Herr Radandt. I wonder if we might have a word with you."

It wasn't exactly a question. "Of course." Ernst pointed to the chairs on his front porch. "It's a beautiful day. Perhaps you'd like to sit outside and enjoy the fresh air."

Actually it was a bit cold, but the men didn't argue. They bundled up their coats, and each took a seat. "Herr Radandt, you have two sons, is that right?"

"Yes. And two daughters."

"Your daughters are of no concern to us. We want to talk to you about your sons. Ernst-August and Friedhelm."

Ernst nodded. This wasn't an idle visit. They knew the names of his boys. "Go on," he told them.

"They are very impressive boys. The Hauptjungzugführer who heads up the local Jungvolk has spoken very highly of them. We have no doubt Ernst-August will do very well when he matriculates to the Hitlerjugend later this year."

"Thank you," Ernst told them. All boys were required to become members of the paramilitary Hitler Youth upon their fourteenth birthdays. Ernst didn't like it, but he said the words he was expected to say. "He is lucky to have the opportunity."

"On the contrary: we are lucky to have him. He's a brave and clever boy. We also took the liberty of looking into your younger son, Friedhelm. Quite a bright and alert little boy, isn't he? You must be very proud."

"Indeed I am," Ernst answered.

"Are you familiar with the Napola schools?"

Ernst nodded. The *Nationalpolitische Lehranstalt*, Napola for short, were military boarding schools created by Hitler to produce future leaders steeped in Nazi ideology. They were also known for harsh discipline and rigorous training.

"We would very much like your boys to join us as cadets. We think that with the right education, your sons will grow into great men."

Ernst considered carefully his options for how to reply to these men, these dangerous Nazis who had come to his home while he was giving thanks to God and now said they wanted to take his sons.

He took a deep breath and watched it turn to fog as it hit the cold air.

"It is a great honor for your sons to be invited to the Napola," said the older of the two, who seemed to be the one in charge. "But if it is too much of a hardship to relinquish both of your boys, then give us the younger. Give us Friedhelm."

Because, Ernst knew, it is easier to indoctrinate a younger boy.

"No," he told them. "No, I will not. These are my sons, and I am responsible for their education."

The two Nazis looked at one another. It was obvious they weren't used to being turned down. "Are you quite sure?"

"My sons will not attend your Napola school."

The Nazis stood. "That is a regrettable answer, Herr Radandt—as you will no doubt discover. Best wishes to your boys. Enjoy the rest of your day."

Ernst watched the men as they left. He was unsure what he had just done. It was 1944. The Nazis were very practiced by now at handling dissent, and they weren't known for their mercy. Would they come back for him? Would they take him away, as they had already taken away so many others?

It was possible.

Ernst stepped back inside the house, shivering from the cold. His friends were waiting for him, and they wanted to know what had happened with the Nazis. "What did they want? What did you say to them?"

But Ernst didn't want to talk about it. He wanted to pray.

That week, at work, he learned that he was to be reassigned out of the recruitment office in Neustettin. The orders weren't yet final, but he was told that he would be stationed somewhere on the Eastern Front, in the war against Russia.

The war in the east had been going very badly for the Germans. No one knew *how* badly, exactly—the information was clouded with propaganda—but the front line was collapsing, and casualties numbered in the millions. Those who weren't killed in battle faced even worse horrors if they were captured.

The Eastern Front was a death sentence.

Ernst thought of the two smug Nazi officials walking off his porch that Sunday afternoon, safe and comfortable as they manipulated the lives and livelihoods of so many innocent people who were simply trying to go about their lives.

The Eastern Front. As a recruitment officer, Ernst himself had known many soldiers who were shipped off to the Eastern Front. He had seen them in those moments after they'd learned where they were to be stationed, as reinforcements for the armies outside Leningrad or Stalingrad or in the steppes of the Ukraine. They said good-bye to their families. Some of them even tried to put on happy faces when they boarded the train. But they knew they might never return.

And many of them never did.

A regrettable decision, the Nazi had called Ernst's answer to their offer. Ernst thought about it again and again, as he waited to receive his official orders, but he never regretted his decision. *These are my sons, and I am responsible for their education*, he repeated to himself. *And that means I will teach them by my example to stand for their convictions and do what is right.*

Ernst began making preparations for the time when he would no longer be in Neustettin. He tilled the garden in the spring and planted a new crop of vegetables so his family would have food at harvest time. He spent as much free time as he could spare with his family, playing with his children and helping them with their studies.

Gisela would be turning sixteen very soon, and at that age the Nazi regime required girls to complete a *Pflichtjahr*—one year of obligatory training in farming and household duties, for the good of the Fatherland. It was important to Ernst that he find Gisela a good home for her Pflichtjahr. He reached out to many of his friends and acquaintances on the farms around Pomerania and finally arranged for her to stay on the estate of Rittergut Dolgen, not far from Neustettin, where she would be a nanny for the well-to-do Schütze family, looking after their two children. Mr. Schütze had assured Ernst that he and his wife would do everything in their power to guarantee Gisela's safety and would flee ahead of the Russian army, should it come to that. Ernst could tell that Mr. Schütze was not a friend of the Nazis. He was greatly relieved to have found such a good match.

Ernst was a soldier in the army, and he would go wherever they ordered him to go. But he had also spent many years in Neustettin, and he'd made a lot of friends there and earned a lot of trust. One such friend was a high-ranking military officer who came to visit Ernst that spring.

"I have new orders for you, my friend. The army needs you to ship out. Start packing your things. And Ernst—pack for a warm climate."

Ernst didn't understand. "A warm climate?"

"I hope you weren't excited about fighting in Russia. I've arranged to have you sent to Italy. You'll join a company in Pavia, for an office job."

Ernst couldn't believe what he heard. It took a moment before he grasped the full impact of this unexpected order, before joy flooded his mind. He had circumvented the Nazis yet again. He wouldn't be going to the Eastern Front after all. He was going to Italy.

He smiled and saluted. "Yes, sir."

"*Arrivederci*," the officer said.

"*Arrivederci*," Ernst replied.

CHAPTER 12

PORTA WESTFALICA: 1944

"DEAR EVELINE," LUDWIG started the letter.

Beginning was easy enough. He liked writing the shape of his wife's name. *Eveline.* It comforted him to see it. But then he drew the comma, and he stalled. He wasn't sure how to continue. His pen hovered over the blank page as he waited for the right words to come until the ink started drying in the nib.

There was much that he wanted to tell his wife, but putting his feelings into words was never easy for him. In the months since he'd left his family behind in Warsaw, Ludwig had disappeared even deeper into his work, and it had kept him so busy lately that he felt a bit estranged from himself.

"I am very much looking forward to seeing you and the children this summer. I have applied for a furlough that should allow us to reunite, albeit only briefly."

The past few months had been hard on Ludwig—very hard, but also very reassuring. He had learned about the death threat from the Polish resistance. The leaders of the Polish Underground State had decided that the Philips Corporation, and Ludwig's work there, were too important to the Nazi war effort to be allowed to continue unchecked. There was no room for bargaining: they had decided that he needed to be eliminated.

But some of them also knew Ludwig personally. They knew he had many Polish friends and that he had, on occasion, stood up for them and their interests against the Nazis. He was, they decided, one of the "good Germans."

Because of this, they deemed it appropriate to warn him. Two men had approached him one afternoon as he stepped off the train and let him know in no uncertain terms that if he stayed in Poland, he would be killed. But if he were willing to leave, they would give him the opportunity to get out of harm's way.

When Ludwig arrived home a bit later that day, he was deep in thought, wishing he could keep the news of the death threat from Eveline. He prayed for guidance. Once the children were sleeping, he opened up to his wife, who remained unusually calm as they talked together. What would be the best way to get out of Warsaw? Would management at Philips believe him? Would he have to resign his position? Ludwig knew all along that he had only one choice. He would talk to his superiors in the morning.

The Polish resistance had been growing in strength and in confidence. Their efforts to sabotage the German military were inflicting real, effective damage upon the Nazis, and they were getting even more brazen as the Germans' Eastern Front moved west out of Russia and closer to the Polish border. The fortunes of the war were turning, so the management at the Philips Corporation had every reason to take the threat to Ludwig's life seriously.

They agreed that it would be best, at least for the time being, to transfer Ludwig out of Poland to a safer location inside Germany. Ludwig packed hastily, said good-bye to his family, and boarded an evening train. He had been told to make his way to Porta Westfalica and given a contact number there. Where exactly he was going, he did not know.

He arrived the next morning at an old abandoned mining site.

Though it hadn't been an active mine for many years, the place was humming with activity.

A soldier greeted him at the gate. "Welcome to Porta Westfalica, Herr Job."

The Allied bombing of industrial Germany had been relentless over the past months, and the German government had seized on the old mines of Porta Westfalica as a place to build sheltered, underground production facilities for all its vitally needed equipment. A dozen stories below ground, they were assembling factories for aircraft engines, oil refineries, and military communication equipment—including, of course, radio tubes.

Ludwig Job was assigned an office in the research laboratories on the ninth floor . . . underground.

He took up a temporary residence close to the mine and settled into a new routine. He woke early, same as always, walked from his home to the complex, greeted the soldiers at the front gate, and rode the slow elevator down into the darkness. On the days he worked late, he barely saw sunlight at all. If the Polish resistance had wanted him removed from working for the German war effort, they had failed. Now, more than ever, he was surrounded by activities that exclusively were to benefit the military on the battlefield. He saw workers from a nearby concentration camp arrive at the mine daily, and he saw SS soldiers supervising those workers as they did the hard work of digging deeper into the abandoned mine to create production facilities. Ludwig didn't want to think about what he saw. Instead, he stayed to himself in his lab, thankful that his life had been spared in Warsaw and that he still had a job with Philips that kept him from being drafted into the military.

Eveline was good at writing letters. She had, after all, been a student of literature at the university. She wrote to him often. She described her days, which were spent carrying on the daily routines with the four children in his absence. She wrote about how long and challenging those days sometimes were, but she also reminded him how comforted she was knowing that he was safe—safe from the Polish Resistance, and safe from the front lines where so many of their friends and family faced grave danger. Ludwig's three brothers, all raised in Poland, were stationed on the Eastern Front, and the family lived in constant fear of news that they had been wounded or killed in action. The Soviets were getting closer, and the Polish resistance was getting more active and violent. "But for now," she wrote, "everyone is safe. Everyone is missing you."

He tried to reply in kind with reassuring words. "I've found a Baptist church in a town nearby called Bad Oeynhausen," he wrote. "As you can imagine, I am attending worship services there on Sundays. The people have become my friends."

In a way, joining with fellow Baptists on Sundays gave Ludwig an opportunity for a few hours to escape his growing uneasiness with the war and with the Nazi regime. Living in Warsaw during the harsh German occupation had given him insights into their cruel methods and their inhumanity. It had been hard for him to watch his fellow countrymen being mistreated and their country being robbed of its history and its culture. He had come to admire the commitment of the Polish resistance fighters, even though due to circumstances not under their control he had become one of their targets. There was nobody at work, in his underground office and lab setup, with whom he could talk about these matters. He was terribly alone. The Baptist church in Bad Oeynhausen proved to be an effective antidote to that loneliness. Its members invited him for Sunday dinner, and together they enjoyed great discussions about matters of faith and also how badly the war was going, particularly in Russia. That was where the conversation stopped. They stayed away from talking about Hitler and the Nazis.

But during the week, the long days of darkness and the worrisome news he heard each day on the radio were taking a toll on him. He tuned his radio to any news he could get from Poland. It helped him to feel more at home in his underground laboratory, and when he was lost in work with Polish voices playing on the radio in the background, he could even imagine that he was still at home, close to his family.

"It would be best for all of us," he wrote, "if we were to plan a trip for this summer. Let's get some country air. Let's get the children out of Warsaw."

Ludwig's family still had the farm where he had grown up in Gross-Grabina, and he liked to take any opportunity to visit. The contrast to city life was striking, and even short visits did much to revitalize him.

The farm had passed from Ludwig's father to his brother Richard, but Richard decided that farming life was not for him and turned it over to their younger brother, Eduard. Eduard and his wife, Ruth, were perfectly suited to carry on the two-hundred-year history of the Job family farm, and they maintained it together until Eduard was drafted into the army. Now Ruth managed the farm with the help of Ludwig's mother, Emilie.

Ludwig's children loved the farm. They had spent their summer vacation there in 1943. They loved watching, petting, and feeding the animals.

"What's your favorite animal?" Ludwig asked them.

Eduard liked the cows. "I think we have a connection," he said. He would lean on the fence and watch them as they chewed their cud, and they would watch him watch them, slow and serious.

Georg liked chasing the ducks and geese around the yard. He wanted them to make it across the sandy road into the pond. But they would just squawk and run from him until they lost patience with the game, and then they would turn around and chase him, and he would run away in terror.

Elizabeth's favorite animal was the fox.

"The fox?" Ludwig asked. "There are no foxes here!"

"Yes there are, Daddy!" She excitedly took him by the hand and walked with him out to the nearby woods, where Ludwig was surprised to discover she was right! There were foxholes not more than a hundred yards from the farmhouse. “Maybe if we’re very quiet, they’ll come out to play,” he told her, and they hid behind a log for a few minutes, waiting to see if any of the foxes would come out of their den.

But Elizabeth got impatient. “We can look for foxes later. Now it’s time for lunch!”

Sometimes the children piled into the back of one of the farm’s horse-drawn wagons and rode it along the bumpy, unpaved country roads, singing songs in warbling voices until they collapsed in laughter.

Other days, they packed food baskets full of sandwiches and filled cups full of grain coffee and brought them to the Polish workers out in the fields.

Ludwig loved watching his children explore the farm the way he had as a boy. He loved pointing out its little details, secrets that time had nearly forgotten—the old foundation of the original farmhouse, the row of trees he had planted as a boy that were now taller than any of the buildings, a shed that he and his brothers had constructed.

There was also a barn door where the Job children through the ages had charted their growth, a collection of brightly colored hash marks noted with a name and a date. Ludwig showed his children the marks he had made when he was their age, and they stood next to the marks to see if they were taller or shorter than their father had been.

“Can we add our names too?” Elizabeth asked him.

“Of course you can. You are Jobs, after all.”

This farm had been his home, and he wanted his children to feel the place was their home too. From here, it was easy to forget that the world was at war. And that was exactly how he wanted his children to spend their summer.

From his underground lab in Porta Westfalica, he wrote to his wife, “I will come to Warsaw this summer so I can deliver the children to the farm at Gross-Grabina. Warsaw will be safe enough for me now, at least to visit. The resistance has more important things to focus on these days than a humble radio researcher.”

Now that the date for his death sentence had passed, he knew that the Polish resistance would require a new secret trial before they would put his name back on the list of those sentenced to death, so there was no significant risk for him in visiting his family in Warsaw.

Ludwig's managers approved his furlough, and in early July, for the first time since he'd fled Warsaw that winter, he boarded the train out of Porta Westfalica to go home.

He didn't even realize how exhausted he had been all those months until he spent his first night sleeping in his own bed next to his wife. And when young Waldemar's crying woke them in the middle of the night, Ludwig greeted the sound with nothing but joy.

He traveled with his three older children out of Warsaw to the farm in Gross-Grabina, all of them growing giddy with excitement as they left the city limits. Eveline had stayed behind with Waldemar. It was too hard to travel with the toddler, and they thought it would be imprudent for them to leave their house completely empty with so much unrest in the city. Ludwig helped his three children settle in at the farm with their grandmother, Emilie, and their Aunt Ruth.

It was the perfect place for his children to spend their summer. They were in the best of care possible under the circumstances of war-torn Poland. On Sundays, they would accompany their grandmother and their aunt to services at the German Baptist Church in Dąbie, where several generations of Jobs in Grabina had gone to the church and where Ludwig himself had been baptized.

A few days later, he said good-bye to them. He needed to return to his underground laboratory in Germany.

"But I want you to stay!" Elizabeth cried.

He knelt and kissed her head. "I want to stay too, but I can't. I need you to take care of the cows and the chickens and the goats for me until I come back at the end of August. Then we'll all go home to your mother, just in time for you to go back to school. What do you think of that?"

That was Ludwig's plan when he boarded the train and headed back to Porta Westfalica in July. But as the summer wore on, Ludwig listened to the radio news and began to realize he might need a different plan. The Soviets were drawing closer and closer to Warsaw. Then, on August 1, *Armia Krajowa*, the Polish Home Army, rose up against the Nazi occupation and open fighting broke out in the streets.

Ludwig quickly had new travel papers drawn up and signed, and he boarded a train back to Poland. Upon his arrival home, he greeted his alarmed wife at the door with two empty suitcases. "Surprise!" He gave her a tired smile. "I'm home!"

They agreed that it wasn't safe for them to stay in Warsaw. They would head west to the town of Kalisz, a relatively short distance from Gross-Grabina, where Richard had an apartment with his wife, Emma. Kalisz was part of the Polish territory that had been annexed to the Warthegau, the new German district where Hitler had decided to set up a model Nazi state. Eveline and the four children would seek shelter there, away from the Polish uprising and the Red Army, and in the fall the three older children would enroll in school, where for the first time in their lives every morning began with the "Heil Hitler!" salute. Elizabeth found it strange. When asked by her mom how the first day of school had gone, she asked why they had to say "Heil Hitler." Eveline told her it would be best to do as the other children were doing.

Before leaving Warsaw, the Jobs packed their silverware, their crystal vases and bowls, their best dishes, their clothing, and even a cherished encyclopedia and shipped them to Kalisz, where they planned to retrieve them. But at the rail station, Ludwig got nervous seeing all their valuables gathered up in one place and decided, on a hunch, to split the shipment and send half to the Philips corporate office in Hamburg. *This may be more trouble than it's worth*, he thought, *but better safe than sorry.*

They grabbed one last bundle of luggage and left their still-furnished apartment, unpacked clothes scattered everywhere, oil paintings still covering the walls.

"Will we ever be back here?" Eveline asked her husband. There was no way for him to answer. She kissed him on the cheek and closed and locked the door.

Eveline went ahead to Kalisz with the baby while Ludwig traveled to Gross-Grabina to fetch his other children.

"Daddy!" Elizabeth greeted him. "Is it already time for us to go home?"

"No, Elizabeth," he told her. "We're not going home."

Though Ludwig couldn't know it then, they would never go home again.

CHAPTER 13

POMERANIA: 1944

ON JUNE 17, 1944, Ernst-August Radandt turned fourteen and graduated from the Nazi organization for boys, the Deutsches Jungvolk, and into the paramilitary Hitlerjugend. The Hitlerjugend was mandatory for all German boys between the ages of fourteen and eighteen, to give them a solid foundation in military training and Nazi doctrine and to facilitate their transformation into soldiers when they turned eighteen.

Because of Ernst-August's exemplary record with the Jungvolk, and because of the pluck he showed upon joining the Hitlerjugend, his commanders immediately recommended him for special training at the Motorsportführer Schule. They wanted him to learn how to ride a motorcycle. The boy was too young, officially, to join the war effort as a soldier, and his father had refused to enroll him in one of the Nazi Napola boarding schools—but they knew there would be other ways to put this brave and diligent boy to use.

Ernst-August loved the motorcycle. He loved riding fast on an open road, the roar of the engine underneath him and the roar of the wind around him, tossing his blond hair. To him, driving the motorcycle felt like flying, or as close to flying as he would ever come. Once he was well practiced enough that he was allowed to leave the school's closed course and drive out onto the country roads outside Neustettin, he would gun the throttle as he climbed the hills, trying to hit the crest with enough speed to hurl the bike into the air so he'd really be flying, for a second or two, before touching down again with a rough bounce and a squeal of tires on the downhill side of the road.

As part of his training, he needed to log a certain number of miles on the bike, so he took longer and longer trips to the countryside, to places he'd never visited before. The rural roads twisted and forked, and each time he chose one direction he would make a mental note to go back later and explore the other road too. Before long, he knew most of the back roads throughout the county.

The Motorsportführer Schule wanted its students to be able to handle motorcycles in the harshest conditions. They had Ernst-August ride on obstacle courses of dirt and gravel and cobblestones, down stairs and through narrow alleys. They sent him out to ride in the worst wind and rain. The instructors also created some of the conditions of war, yelling at the boys through bullhorns, chasing them, and throwing rocks. A few times they even pointed and fired guns that were loaded with blanks so the boys could acclimate to frightening situations in a safer, simulated environment. The time would come soon enough when they would have to face those same conditions on actual battlefields.

The school warned its students: accidents on a motorcycle will happen, just like accidents on a bicycle or on skis are inevitable. It was a matter of *when*, not *if*. What was important, then, was to learn how to behave during a crash so the driver could do everything in his power to limit his injuries. The boys learned that there were right and wrong ways to fall from the motorcycle. They practiced overbalancing their bikes at slow speeds until they tipped over, discovering the limits of what was possible. Ernst-August practiced using the frame of his motorcycle to help shield his body from a crash and learned how to avoid burning himself on the hot tailpipe if the motorcycle tipped onto him. He learned when it was prudent to slow the bike sharply with its brakes and when, in other conditions, it was safer not to use the brakes at all and thus avoid skidding, crashing, or going over the handlebars.

He quickly became an adept driver. His love for the motorcycle showed. He passed the course at the Motorsportführer Schule with flying colors and was promoted to *Oberscharführer*, group leader. Then, because of his aptitude with the motorcycle, the leaders at the Hitlerjugend recommended him for the Nationalsozialistisches Kraftfahrkorps, the NSKK, a Nazi paramilitary organization in charge of transportation. On August 6, 1944, Ernst-August was drafted into the NSKK, given a new uniform and a new title—*Rottenführer*—and moved out of his family's home and into one of the barracks in Neustettin.

It was not even two months after his fourteenth birthday.

Ernst-August's particular assignment was to carry orders, including secret orders, to different units and commanders in the region. He also had to pick up copies of different newspapers from a bookstore in the small town of Bublitz, located a short distance north of Neustettin, and deliver them to his commander, Herr Schreiber.

He loved the trips to Bublitz and the chance to explore some of the areas outside the county limits of Neustettin. The bookstore in Bublitz was run by a woman who had gone to school with Ernst-August's mother, Gertrud, and the woman would ask about his family every time he visited. But he rarely had time to chat. "Everyone's doing well," he'd answer quickly as he stuffed the newspapers into his satchel. "See you next week!"

Then he'd open the throttle of his motorcycle and set off again through the country roads.

When he arrived back in town, sometimes he would see girls from his school watching him as he drove past. He would smile at them and rev the engine a little louder as he went by. They would always smile back. Ernst-August was starting to learn what these girls already knew: he was handsome and charming and effortlessly deft at talking to just about anyone—even teenage girls.

Most of Ernst-August's motorcycle trips were back and forth to the *Ostwall*, an embankment built to help fortify the town against attack. Ever since springtime, the citizens of Neustettin had been going by bus to the outer perimeter of the town, to the fields on its east side, and once they got there, they would dig.

The government had enlisted all able bodies to help with the construction of the Ostwall, which was part of a much larger bulwark that had been built up before the war, originally to help defend against the envisioned possibility of a Polish invasion.

In July of 1944, the NSKK was tasked with reinforcing the Ostwall so the German army could hold off the advancing Russian front. The engineers mapped out plans to build up the wall, to add new bunkers and platforms to its structure, and to dig special trenches called *Panzersperren*, designed to impede incoming tanks.

Townspeople were recruited to work on the project. They were bussed to the site, handed shovels, and told where to dig. Many were housed at the site for weeks or even months, focusing their work on the Panzersperren, the "tank traps." If the ditches were deep enough and the embankment high enough, the engineers reasoned, then any oncoming tanks would flip over and be rendered useless.

The construction of these "tank traps" consumed the town for many months, and Ernst-August made many trips back and forth between the town and various construction sites of the Ostwall, delivering messages and placing requests for different materials with local vendors and volunteer coordinators.

The engineers in charge were always making adjustments to their designs, based on whatever they had managed to find out from similar projects in other towns on whatever rumors they had heard about the capabilities of Soviet armor. The trenches needed to be deeper. The walls needed to be higher. The whole structure needed to be reinforced with more beams of wood, with more sandbags, to help it weather the heavy rains. The engineers always needed something new. The construction was constant and ongoing, and it kept the NSKK and the entire town quite busy for many months.

The effort and expenditure would be utterly futile, a colossal waste of time and resources—even Ernst-August could see that. When the Russian tanks did finally arrive in Neustettin early in 1945, they sped straight through the Ostwall without even slowing down.

During his time spent driving the roads outside Neustettin, Ernst-August saw other things that he would not have seen in town. He noticed trucks driving back from the Eastern Front packed with men who were missing arms, missing legs, missing eyes. He would salute the men as he drove past, and sometimes they would salute him back. But not always. Sometimes they just stared off, like they were tired of saluting.

Where were the trucks taking these men? What would happen to them? How would they live with their injuries? And how many more trucks full of wounded soldiers were there throughout Germany?

Some days, on these same roads, Ernst-August encountered long caravans of horse-drawn carriages carrying refugee families—German farmers, mostly—who had packed a small portion of their worldly possessions into wagons and fled westward, driven by fear of the oncoming Red Army. The caravans stretched on and on, sometimes for miles—longer than Ernst-August imagined possible. They were piled with food and blankets and clothing, but mostly just with people—so many poor, desperate people.

"Sir," Ernst-August asked a man driving one of the wagons, "where are you going?"

The man looked at Ernst-August and shrugged. "Away." That was his only answer. "Just away."

These people were frightened to be leaving their homes but even more frightened to stay behind. Better to abandon their farms altogether than to risk what would happen to them if they fell into the hands of the dreaded Russian soldiers.

Back at the barracks, Ernst-August and the other boys in his unit listened to the announcements on the Volksempfänger. The radio was always on, and it was only ever tuned to one station: *Deutschlandsender*, the official German broadcast—"Radio Germany."

The German army was holding strong on the Eastern Front, the radio told them. The Allied offensive in Normandy continued to result in severe British and American casualties. Every wheel was rolling toward German victory.

There had been an assassination attempt on Hitler's life, the radio also said. Some high-ranking officers had set off a bomb inside a barrack of the Führer's headquarters in East Prussia, and the plot might have worked had Hitler not been saved by what he called divine providence. By the end of the summer nearly all of the traitors had been caught, put on trial, found guilty, and hanged. "Hanged," the Führer ordered, "like cattle."

Many of the traitors, Ernst-August realized, were from Pomerania—the place he considered his home. Some of them had been raised on the same farming estates his father Ernst had visited as a young man, estates very much like the one where Ernst-August's sister Gisela was now doing her Pflichtjahr. They'd started out with every advantage, and they'd turned those advantages to treason. Why?

Ernst-August wondered, as he drove the winding country roads outside Neustettin, whom he could trust if his own countrymen were capable of plotting against the Fatherland? He couldn't come up with any reason that would make sense to him. Living as he was in the barracks with some members of the local NSKK troop, a group of about ten, he heard their thoughts and opinions day and night. What he learned from them often stood in stark contrast to what he had been told at home, and sometimes he was unsure what or whom to believe. But he knew it was best if he did not bring up such questions with his new comrades. It was so different from what he had been used to, and there were moments when he actually missed going to school. He missed the friendship he had enjoyed with his schoolmates and even with some of his teachers.

He drove his motorcycle past his family's house at 34 Bugenhagenstrasse. Now that he was living at the barracks, whole days would pass without him seeing them. Some days he wouldn't even think about them. He was too busy. He'd get to the end of a long day, sore in his arms from wrestling with the handlebars of the motorcycle all day long, and be glad to sleep. There wasn't much time to be homesick.

But when he was on an errand that didn't require him to hurry, sometimes he would drive past his house and see if he could steal a glimpse of his family. The house was so empty lately. His father was in Italy, and his sister was with the Schütze family at their estate. Often, Ernst-August would see Friedhelm in the yard—feeding the chickens or raking the autumn leaves or just playing—and if Friedhelm saw him, Ernst-August would salute to his brother as he passed. If he had a little time, he'd get off his bike and join his brother for a few minutes, just like old times.

Today, though, the yard was empty, and Ernst-August felt a pinch of worry in his chest. Where was Friedhelm?

He dropped the kickstand on his motorcycle and ran up to the front of the house. Inside, it was all quiet. Ernst-August realized he hadn't seen his family in days. "Friedhelm? Mother?"

His mother came running down the stairs. "Bubi!" she cried, calling him by his nickname. "I didn't hear you come in. What are you doing here? Is everything all right?"

"Where is Friedhelm?" Ernst-August asked.

"You remember," his mother answered. "He's in Gross-Jestin."

Oh, Ernst-August thought. *Of course.* The summer trip to visit his cousins in Gross-Jestin had originally been planned as a part of Ernst-August's own birthday celebration. The family was going to send him to the country to visit the cousins, making ice cream to sell in Uncle Max's bakery. But instead, Ernst-August had been drafted into the NSKK, and his brother was given the opportunity instead.

"I remember now."

His mother took him into the kitchen and poured him a glass of milk. "Tell me, where have you been today on that motorcycle of yours? Have they sent my little boy on any dangerous missions?" She made no secret of the fact that she didn't approve of the Nazis' decision to recruit children into their war.

"I'm not a little boy anymore. And no, I haven't been anywhere dangerous. Just the Ostwall."

Gertrud nodded. "Everyone is working hard on the Ostwall. They wouldn't be working so hard to build it up, I suppose, unless they were sure that the Russians will advance all the way to Pomerania."

It was a subject that Ernst-August and the others in his barracks weren't very willing to entertain, at least not out loud. But Gertrud persisted.

"If the Russians do get close, I'm going to take your brother and sister to my family in Kolberg, where it's safer. And I think you should join us."

Ernst-August sighed. "Mother, I have a job now. I can't just leave because you want me to. Anyway, you worry too much. The Russians won't come this far. Every wheel is turning toward victory."

The silence hung in the air between them for a moment. "The house gets so quiet now, with all of you gone," Gertrud said, finally.

"I should be getting back." Ernst-August kissed his mother on the cheek and walked out the door. He did miss them all, of course. But he didn't have time to be homesick. With his father stationed in Italy, Ernst-August was the man of the family now, and he needed to get back to work.

He turned the ignition on his motorcycle and smiled as the engine rumbled to life. He loved the sound of it. He kicked the bike into gear and drove off.

CHAPTER 14

KALISZ: DECEMBER 1944

THE SNOW WAS FALLING, and Eveline Job walked with her three-year-old son, Waldemar, and her sister-in-law, Emma Job, through the streets of Kalisz. She tried her best to protect her little boy from the wind and the cold by keeping him bundled up with a scarf she'd made and with his *Fausthandschuhe*, his mittens. But he kept dropping them on the street. She would look down to see his little fingers turning blue in the cold.

"Where is your mitten?" she would ask him. He'd look back up at her and shrug.

Then the three of them would walk together, Eveline's hand clutched tightly around Waldemar's so he'd stay close and keep up and not wander off, and also to help warm his hand against the cold. They would retrace their steps through town until she found the mitten, lying in the middle of the sidewalk or in the street, and she would pull it back over his hand.

"You need to be more careful!" she would warn him.

Then, within minutes, it would happen again.

"Waldemar!"

She didn't know if he was dropping them by accident or if this was his idea of a game. But she didn't have time for this.

"It's just his age," Emma consoled her. "He'll outgrow it."

She looked down at the boy. "Yes, if he doesn't freeze to death first." She tied a knot in Waldemar's scarf to try to secure it, and he immediately began pulling at the knot with his restless fingers.

"Waldemar!"

He looked up at her with innocent eyes. "What, Mama?" He didn't even know he was doing it.

She scooped him into her arms to carry him the rest of the way. He was almost too big to hold, but it was the only way they would have a chance to make it across town in time.

"Elizabeth was never like this," Eveline confided to Emma as she shifted Waldemar from one arm to the other.

Seven-year-old Elizabeth was the reason Eveline was desperate to get across town. It was only two days until Christmas, and though Eveline had already found gifts for Eduard, Georg, and Waldemar, she had something special in mind for her little girl, and she wouldn't rest until she had found it.

She wanted Elizabeth to have a doll.

All of Elizabeth's dolls had been left behind or lost during the Jobs' sudden move from Warsaw the past summer. Elizabeth claimed not to mind much, but Eveline remembered what it was like to be a seven-year-old girl. She had been Elizabeth's age when her family was exiled from Poland to Omsk, and during those first unsettling months, her dolls had been her best, most loyal friends.

Her children were growing up in a terrible time, Eveline thought to herself. They couldn't fully understand all the turmoil around them—why they were so far from home, why they had changed schools, or why this new school required them to begin each day with a "Heil Hitler!" They didn't understand why their father couldn't be with them, why food was sometimes so scarce, or why there were so many horse-drawn carriages filled with refugees and so many sad, scared people filing through the town.

Eveline knew, of course, that these circumstances were well beyond her ability to change. But if she could make her children even a little bit happier, or ease their worries in any way, then she was going to do it.

"We are getting the doll tonight," she announced to Emma. There was a shop in town that had a beautiful porcelain doll in its display window, with blue eyes, delicate fingers, long braided hair, and a lace dress with matching gloves. "How late do you think the shop will be open?"

Emma didn't look hopeful. "You know they will need to have their lights out before sunset." Like many areas across the Warthegau, Kalisz was on guard to shut out its lights at nighttime and cover its windows to keep light from leaking out, in order to try to hide the town from the view of Allied bombers.

"We'll make it," Eveline said confidently.

She had been in Kalisz with the children for nearly half a year now—long enough to have learned a few shortcuts across town. She led them off the main street and took a back street she knew well, the same route she took each Sunday morning on her way to the German Baptist Church of Kalisz, which the family had been attending since their arrival in town in August.

Outside the church, there was a refugee family taking shelter from the wind—a mother and two children—and they were huddling under a small wool blanket. They nodded to Eveline. "Good evening," the woman said.

"It would be an even better evening," Eveline answered, "if you weren't out here in the cold."

"Oh, it's not so bad, now that this church is shielding us from the wind."

Eveline looked at the family. It was just the woman, wearing a warm fur hat, a boy who looked to be ten, and girl whose face below a knitted cap was framed with two strips of braided hair. She reminded Eveline of her own Elizabeth. "Is your husband in the war?" Eveline asked.

A shadow fell over the woman's face, and she hugged her two children a little closer to her. "He was in the war. Now he's buried in the ground, in a place called Vitebsk. In the Balkans."

"I'm very sorry to hear that."

Eveline was at a loss whenever she spoke to these war widows. Invariably, they would ask her where her own husband was fighting—was he also on the Eastern Front? And then she would explain that no, her husband wasn't a soldier. He was a scientist. He was doing very important research in a secret laboratory underground, somewhere in Germany.

"Well, he must be very important indeed, to be safe underground," they would say to her, and whatever rapport Eveline might have had with these women would be gone, wiped out by this one fundamental difference in their situations. Her husband was alive and theirs weren't.

Ludwig was very important. Eveline knew this to be true. But she had also come to understand that the real difference between herself and these widows had very little to do with her husband's importance.

"This is my church," Eveline said abruptly. "I'm afraid there isn't room for you to stay with us at our apartment, because we're already housing some soldiers there. But I know the pastor here, and if you like, I can ask him if he might offer you shelter for the night."

The refugee woman was very proud, and she looked as if she might shrug off Eveline's offer. But then she suddenly burst into tears. "It's been a while since anyone has offered us a kindness."

"Stay here," Eveline told the woman. "I'll be right back."

Emma and Waldemar waited with the family while Eveline went off in the direction of the clergy house. The pastor was just sitting down to dinner. "Bring them over," he agreed. "We'll set a few more places at the table. They can even join us for a hot meal."

By the time Eveline made it back to the family at the church, the sun had set over Kalisz, and the shopkeepers were locking their doors for the evening. "I guess we're not going to make it to that shop today, after all,"

Emma said with a frown, though both women knew they had made the right choice about how to spend their evening.

"It's just a doll, right?"

Ludwig would arrive in Kalisz tomorrow on an evening train. Eveline knew that he was planning to buy some presents for the children before he left Bad Oeynhausen. With any luck, maybe he'd bring a doll for Elizabeth.

"God bless you," the refugee woman said to them as they parted ways.

"God bless you and your family," Eveline said sincerely, and she thanked the pastor too, for taking the refugees in on this bitter night. Then she and Emma and Waldemar set off again through town in the wind and the cold.

Then she looked down at her son.

"Waldemar! Where is your scarf?"

She couldn't believe it. After everything else that had happened that night—after specifically telling him to be more careful and after tying it in a double-knot around his neck—the boy's knit scarf was nowhere to be seen.

He looked sheepishly at his Aunt Emma, who answered on his behalf. "Waldemar asked me if it would be okay for him to give his scarf to the refugee family."

"Really?"

"Really. Like mother, like son, apparently. I promise I'll knit him a new one."

Eveline smiled at her little boy. "Well, let's hurry home and get out of this cold, then."

They wound their way back toward the apartment, deciding to walk along the now-quiet main street, where the storefronts were shuttered and dark for the night. A snow had started to fall, dusting the sidewalk in an as-yet-unbroken blanket of white.

"Unbelievable," Eveline muttered. Ahead of them the lamplight from one shop leaked out onto the street, glowing extra bright against the snow. It was the shop with the doll in the window.

They tapped on the glass, and the shopkeeper let them in out of the cold. "I seem to have lost track of time," he explained. "What a beautiful night it's turned into."

The doll sat in the display window, exactly as Eveline remembered.

"What a beautiful night indeed," she said, and she left the shop that evening with a crisp, brown parcel tucked under her arm.

PART 2

CHAPTER 15

KALISZ: JANUARY 1945

THE KNOCK CAME in the middle of the night, after Eveline had already put the children to bed. They had wanted to stay up with her. Eduard and Georg, nine and eight years old, were particularly restless. They were full of questions that she didn't know how to answer.

It was January 20, 1945. Ludwig had been home briefly for a few days around Christmas—their first Christmas as refugees—but he'd long since left again, returning via the series of trains that ferried him back to the Philips laboratory in Porta Westfalica. She felt so terribly alone, with so much responsibility to bear for the safety of her family.

She wasn't alone, though. The apartment was full—overfull. She and Emma and the children were sharing the space with a small squad of German soldiers who were stationed there. The soldiers were part of a larger battalion taking temporary cover in Kalisz from the onslaught of the advancing Russians. All the German citizens of the Warthegau were expected to contribute the use of their homes and other resources to the war effort, and Eveline and Emma had been asked to give over the first floor of their apartment to house a German officer and three of the men under his command.

Eveline's boys were fascinated with the soldiers. They'd seen plenty of military men in Warsaw, but never this close or for this long. The boys followed the soldiers around the apartment, watching them, mimicking some of their gruff manners, stomping on the floor, shoving at one another, and even learning a few new German words that Eveline would just as soon wish they had not.

The boys asked the soldiers relentless questions—questions about their uniforms and their guns and what it was like to be in battle, and if they were afraid of the Russians. They asked the soldiers if they had ever killed anyone, but the men always laughed and avoided answering, and Eveline scolded her sons for asking such questions.

When the soldiers weren't around, Eduard and Georg would pretend to be soldiers themselves, defending the apartment from the Red Army, shooting with imaginary rifles through the windows, taking cover from fabricated artillery and grenades by diving behind the sofa or inside the "bunker" of the wardrobe.

For her part, Eveline befriended the soldiers too. The officer sometimes joined the family upstairs for dinner or tea, when his schedule permitted, and like her boys, Eveline asked the officer questions—though out of politeness, she often tried to avoid talking about the war. She reasoned that he'd had plenty of war without her going on about it. Instead, she asked him about his hometown, his wife, and his life before he became a soldier, and he would tell stories about Germany, the country that had been in her conversation and imagination for as long as she could remember but which she'd never seen. He would laugh and joke, and sometimes, just for a moment, he would seem to forget all about the war.

Eveline didn't need to ask him if he was afraid of the Russians, because she could tell that he was. They all were. These soldiers had seen the Red Army advance in what seemed like unlimited numbers, horde after fearless horde, and no German defense was strong enough to withstand the indefatigable Soviet onslaught. A front line that had once reached nearly to Moscow had been pushed back into Belarus and the Ukraine, then pushed back again into Poland. The German army had been retreating now for nearly a thousand miles.

So while they sat sipping tea, reminiscing about more peaceful times, Eveline mostly just wanted to know about the Russians: How far away were they? How quickly were they coming?

They were questions she never voiced.

"Thank you for another wonderful meal," the officer said politely.

She wanted to ask, *Am I safe here with my family?* Eduard and Georg were in the next room, playing again at being soldiers, *ratt-a-tatting* with pretend guns and jabbing at the air with pretend bayonets.

"It's our pleasure," she said.

Pretend Russian bombs began raining down around them, and they finished the meal in awkward silence.

But on the evening of January 20, the officer provided Eveline with the answer to her unspoken questions. "The Russians are very close now. It would be best if you and your family were to leave Kalisz. It is not safe for you to stay."

"When?" she asked.

"Tomorrow."

A funny thought popped into her head: she couldn't evacuate tomorrow. "Tomorrow is my birthday," she told the officer.

He smiled. "Then please give yourself a gift and evacuate."

She nodded, thanked him, and said good night. As soon as she closed the door, she thought of Ludwig, underground in his lab in Porta Westfalica. If she fled Kalisz with the children tomorrow, how would she get word to her husband? There wasn't time for her to post a letter, and even if there were, she couldn't tell him where they were going: they were fleeing without a destination.

She remembered the refugee families who had been passing regularly through town now for months—poor, unfortunate families in caravans headed west with no home, no destination, and no goal except to stay ahead of the Red Army and maybe to fall into the hands of the British or American troops. Many of them had been separated from their loved ones and had no way to find one another. And she remembered that Elizabeth, coming home from school a week or so earlier, had wanted to know from her why so many farmers drove their wagons through the main street of Kalisz: "The wagons are filled with women and children, many without any cover against the snow. They are freezing in those wagons. Where are they going?"

Eveline thought it best to answer honestly and counter the propaganda they were told in school. "Elizabeth, these farmers are leaving their villages because they do not feel safe. They want to get away from the war."

Elizabeth had surprised her by asking back: "Then why aren't we leaving?" It was not a question Eveline was prepared to tackle, but it was something that had made her uneasy for quite some time.

Thank God, Eveline thought. *Thank God for this officer letting us know. Thank God the children are here and we are all together. Thank God Ludwig is safe, and thank God I know how and where to find him later, once we've escaped.*

Were they really fleeing tomorrow? It didn't seem real, yet, but it was. It was very frighteningly real.

She put the children to bed. They were excited and didn't want to sleep, and though she hadn't said anything to them about the officer's news, still she wondered if somehow they had picked up on her agitation, wondered if somehow they understood what was about to happen. But then she saw the boys and Elizabeth giggling and whispering and realized they were secretly scheming some sort of morning surprise for her birthday.

"What are you three talking about?" she asked playfully.

"Nothing!" they called back in unison.

She looked at them, so joyous and innocent and free. All this terror around them, and somehow they'd come through it unblemished.

She hugged them close to her until they twisted and turned and wriggled free. "It's my birthday! Can't I hug my children on my birthday?"

"It's not your birthday until tomorrow!" Eduard reminded her. "You can hug us tomorrow."

She calmed them down and tucked them in. Since Christmas, Elizabeth had been sleeping with her new doll, and she'd already slipped the doll into the bed beside her for the night, its head and little arms poking out from under the covers, its eyes rolled closed. "Sleep, my little daughter," Eveline said, kissing Elizabeth on the forehead.

"Gretel too," Elizabeth demanded. Gretel was the name that Elizabeth had given the doll.

"Sleep, little Gretel," Eveline said to the doll, and she kissed it on its porcelain forehead. Then she pulled the bedroom door closed, and as quietly and discreetly as she could, began packing a few of their things so they would be closer to being ready to evacuate the next day.

She wrote a quick note to Ludwig to let him know they were leaving and addressed it to his office in Porta Westfalica. Maybe she could find a way to mail it before they left town. If not, she would send it as soon as she was able.

What Eveline did not realize was that Ludwig was no longer in Porta Westfalica. Two weeks earlier he had unexpectedly been ordered to the town of Krems, near Vienna, where he was to help oversee the opening of a new Philips plant there. Trucks and freight trains arrived at the location filled with manufacturing equipment, and when they were unloaded, Ludwig knew exactly what needed to be installed where—because it was the same equipment he had used for so many years in Warsaw. When the company shut down the Warsaw plant in the days leading up to the Polish Uprising, it evacuated all of its equipment and relocated it there in Krems. No one knew how to reassemble it all better than Ludwig Job.

They worked long days in Krems, trying to get the new plant up and running. Amid the chaos of recent months, a lot of time and resources had been lost as assets were shuffled around. The hope was that the new plant would be operational before the end of the month, and for that goal to become a reality, all the people involved had to work around the clock.

The night before his wife's birthday, Ludwig surveyed what they'd accomplished so far—an impressive installation in a remarkably short period of time—and the crew took a break to share a few cups of grain coffee. Made from toasted barley and chicory, Ersatzkaffee wasn't much, but they'd all acclimated to its weak flavor.

"I'm surprised you're still here," one of the engineers in Krems told him while they waited for their boiling-hot coffee to cool.

"What do you mean?" Ludwig asked. "I'll be here all week."

"I mean with what's going on in Poland. Isn't your family in Kalisz?"

Ludwig excused himself and switched on the radio. "*Sondermeldung!*" announced the voice on the German news station, but Ludwig grabbed the dial and turned it away from the ever-optimistic German news. He needed facts, not propaganda. He tuned the knob until he found a station broadcasting in Polish. He knew that technically it wasn't legal for him to listen to non-German news, but he also knew that his position as a radio researcher gave him a lot of leeway on that particular rule.

He sat without moving and catalogued in his mind the known positions of the Red Army that were being disclosed by the radio announcer:

Plock.

Lodz.

Czestochowa.

All within just a few hours of his family in Kalisz.

He had to go. He had to go now.

He ran through the plant, looking for a manager with the proper authority to sign him a new set of travel papers. But he couldn't find anyone. They'd all gone home for the day.

"What time is the last train out of Krems?" he asked anyone.

There was too little time.

This is ridiculous, he thought to himself. *I am a manager.* Where the form asked for the signature of his supervisor, to prove that his trip was under orders, he quickly scribbled his own name and hoped no one would look at the papers too closely.

Then he boarded a train out of Krems and began winding his way back northward, toward the front line and his family in Kalisz.

It was late when he arrived, and he realized as he walked up to the apartment that he'd been in such a rush to leave that he'd left his copy of the house key back in the apartment in Porta Westfalica. No choice but to knock.

When Eveline answered, it was hard to tell who was more surprised—she upon seeing her husband, or he upon learning she had already started to pack.

The next morning, the children woke up thinking they needed to get ready for school and were surprised to discover their father sitting at the kitchen table. "You came back for Mommy's birthday!" Elizabeth shouted.

The truth was, with everything else going on, he had all but forgotten about the occasion. But he happily led the children in singing "Happy Birthday" to their mother, and for a few more moments at least, they were a joyful family untroubled by war.

Then the shrill sound of a loudspeaker interrupted them from down on the street. They ran to the window to see a truck with a Nazi swastika on its side and a speaker mounted to its roof, driving up the road announcing to the people of Kalisz a mandatory evacuation by 3:00 p.m. Everyone needed to be out of their homes and headed westward by that afternoon.

Ludwig realized it was by God's grace that he had come home just in time.

"Georg and I will go to the railroad station and find out when we can board a train. Be ready to leave as soon as we get back. Take only what you can carry. Pack clothing, because you will need it. But there will be no room for toys."

With that, Ludwig walked with his son back to the train station he'd just passed through ten hours earlier, this time looking for any opportunity to get his family out of harm's way, perhaps to the city of Stettin.

Elizabeth was in a bother. She packed her bag full of clothes, as her father had instructed, but she didn't know what to do about Gretel. Since Christmas, she and Gretel had been inseparable, and it didn't seem right to leave her behind. Gretel was more important to her than most of her clothes were, and she would happily leave behind a dress or a jacket if it meant being able to travel with her doll.

But her father had been clear: no toys.

Finally, using logic like only a child can, she took the clothes off the doll, folded them up, and packed them into her suitcase. "Clothes are okay, Father said." Then she put Gretel back into her bed and tucked her in, so her head and arms poked out from under the sheets. "Sleep, little Gretel," she said, kissing the doll on its forehead. "I'll come back for you when I can."

Downstairs, there was more knocking at the door. It was the officer who had been living in their parlor. He explained to Eveline and Emma, "Our battalion is leaving within the hour, and you must too, if you are to escape the Soviet Army. There is room in our truck for you and your family, but we must leave now."

"Now?" Eveline asked. "I can't leave now. My husband Ludwig is at the train station, trying to get us tickets."

The soldier looked at his truck, idling by the curb. "Frau Job, there will be no trains out of Kalisz today. If any of us are going to leave this town before the Soviets arrive, that truck is the only way."

Just then the officer's radio chirped with new orders: they were to evacuate Kalisz immediately.

Eveline looked anxiously down the street. Ludwig was nowhere to be seen. "I can't leave," she told the officer. "Not without my husband."

Where was he? What was taking him so long?

Ludwig was frustrated also. The train station and all the streets around it were crowded with people and their luggage, all of them desperate to get out of town. Ludwig quickly saw that nothing at the station was moving; the situation was hopeless. He needed to find another way for his family to escape town.

He realized that if they were going to flee from the Soviets on foot, they'd do better if he could find them a wagon or some other way to manage their luggage and almost four-year-old Waldemar. He ran through the streets, offering to buy a cart or wheelbarrow from one of the other families, but no one would do business with him.

Back at the apartment, the officer and Eveline were screaming at one another. He had already loaded the family's luggage onto his truck. "I cannot wait any longer!" he insisted. "We have to go."

"Then go!" she shouted back. She dragged their luggage off the truck, bag by bag. "I am not leaving here without Ludwig."

"You are being reckless with your family's lives!" he told her, loading her bags back onto the truck.

Twice they did this, back and forth, she obstinately pulling their things off the truck and telling him to leave without her and he wrenching the bags out of her hands and putting them back on.

They both stopped shouting when they saw Ludwig and Georg running up the street, harried and panicked.

"All right, then," Eveline finally conceded to the officer. "We can go."

The whole family climbed aboard the truck, and it pulled away from the curb. By the time Ludwig caught his breath, they were already driving past the city limits of Kalisz, headed west.

Eveline and Emma had one more surprise for everyone: they had managed to use their little free time that morning and their last remaining supplies of butter, flour, and sugar to bake a birthday cake. The family passed pieces of the cake to all the soldiers in the truck, and everyone sang "Happy Birthday" one more time.

Ludwig threw his arm around his wife. "Look at us—we're refugees now. I'm sure this is very far from the best birthday you have ever had."

For a moment, her mind went back to her thirteenth birthday in Omsk, when her family had discussed their exile and whether or not to return to their homeland of Poland. War and politics had dictated her family's moves for almost her entire life.

Eveline rested her head on Ludwig's shoulder and looked at her family, gathered around her in the back of the truck. They were safe, and they were together.

"On the contrary, Ludwig," she said with a soft smile. "This may in fact be the best birthday I have ever had."

CHAPTER 16

NEUSTETTIN: JANUARY 1945

GERTRUD RADANDT SHIFTED impatiently in her seat on the bus and looked out the window for Friedhelm.

The Russian tanks were just outside of Neustettin, or so she had been told, and these busses were lined up in the Hindenburgplatz, the town square, to evacuate a lucky few of the town's citizens. But they had been idling here without moving, running their diesel engines to power the heat while waiting for more people to arrive.

"We won't leave for a couple of hours," a soldier had told her, so she'd sent Friedhelm back to the house to fetch some things she thought were important. They had left the house so quickly, she'd forgotten to grab the suitcase she had packed for her husband.

The twelve-year-old boy said he'd be happy to go get it.

That had been an hour ago, or so she guessed. Really, she had no sense of what time it was. How many hours before dawn? It was the worst, groggiest part of the night. She saw what she thought was a faint glow in the sky from the east, but she didn't know whether it was the early glimmer of the predawn sun, the fiery light of a not-too-distant battlefield, or just her eyes playing tricks on her.

She looked at her daughter Brunhild, asleep in the seat next to her, and then out the window again, up the road toward their house.

Where was he?

She closed her eyes and waited. There was nothing else she could do.

Then, without warning, the bus lurched, closed its door, and growled to life, lumbering from the curb and up the snowy road away from the Hindenburgplatz.

She stood up. "Where are we going?"

But the driver continued on without a word.

"Hey!" She looked around for the soldier who had assured her the bus wouldn't be leaving, but he was nowhere to be seen. "We can't leave yet! My son! My Friedhelm!"

Out the window, the wind was blowing off the lake and whipping the snow into a frenzy. The bus picked up speed, and she watched as the Hindenburgplatz receded in the distance.

She didn't know what to do. Friedhelm was still back there, all alone. She shook the arm of a man in uniform who dozed in a seat nearby. "My son," she said. "We've left him behind!"

The man was only half-awake, but he tried to reassure her. "They will look after him," he said.

"Who? Who will look after him?"

But the man had already fallen back asleep.

She looked back through the window again, watching as the town started to fade away.

"He's only twelve," she said to anyone who was listening.

A few of the other passengers looked back along the road, as if to see if they might spot her lost son, and then they looked at her sadly but didn't know what to say.

The bus rolled up the road and into the countryside.

((•))

Friedhelm turned the corner into the Hindenburgplatz, his arms and legs tired from pulling his sled and his father's suitcase through the snow.

The main road was swathed in trampled snow except for a column of elongated rectangle shapes where the snow had melted and the street showed through, the lingering footprints of the heat from the idling buses.

The buses themselves were nowhere to be seen.

"What a strange day this is turning out to be," he said aloud as he tugged the sled behind him and began walking up the road, heading northwest. Ever since his brother had put on the uniform of a soldier and moved to the barracks, Friedhelm had taken charge of the rabbits and chickens, but also of doing dishes and of keeping the sidewalk clear of snow. He had done so without complaining or whining. Neither would the unknown that now lay ahead of him stop him from moving on. What scared him most was that he felt so alone.

This road, he knew, led to a small village a few kilometers away, and from there, on to Belgard and then Kolberg. His mother had said many times that if they ever needed to evacuate, they would go to Kolberg. Her parents and the other members of the Rattunde family lived there. He knew that was where they would be headed. Of course there was no way he could walk all the way to Kolberg! But at least the road went in the right direction, away from the Russians.

So he walked.

He followed the road along the steep embankment above Lake Streitzig, and when the wind blasted at him, he regretted that he hadn't put on a second sweater. But as he walked, he warmed up, and eventually he didn't notice the cold at all.

It was an oddly calm and beautiful night. The moon was huge in the sky, just a few days past full, and its light bounced off the snow and ice and brightened his path, making it almost clear as day.

Then a truck barreled past him, heading south. And then another, and another. As Friedhelm came to the crest of a hill, he saw that the road ahead of him was heavy with trucks and marching troops, all coming to defend Neustettin. They passed him roughly, either barking at him to get out of their way or barely noticing him. He moved over to the edge of the road, where the snow was deeper, and walked more slowly there, watching his feet.

Soon he came upon another boy, a little older and also dragging a sled. Friedhelm didn't recognize him. Had he gotten separated from one of the refugee caravans?

"Maybe it'd be safer if we walk together," Friedhelm suggested.

The boy shrugged but didn't argue. He didn't seem to want to talk. For the next hour or so, they passed the time in silence, listening to the crunch of their feet on the snowy gravel. Then the boy stopped suddenly.

"I'm thirsty," he announced. "Do you want to stop and eat some snow?"

"Sure," Friedhelm agreed.

By now, there were fewer troops on the road, in smaller numbers and with longer gaps in between.

"I guess that's it for Neustettin," the boy said.

"What do you mean?" asked Friedhelm.

"The Russians will come and wreck everything. Maybe burn it to the ground."

Friedhelm was sure he was wrong. "No, the German army will fight them off."

"You're wrong," the boy told him. "There's no stopping the Russians now. We're lucky we got out when we did. Anyway, those soldiers we saw weren't German. Did you hear them talking? They were Latvian. Latvian SS."

They each bit into their snowballs and let the snow sit in their mouth to warm it up before swallowing.

"How much farther?" the boy asked.

"I don't know," Friedhelm told him. "But I'm getting cold. Let's keep going."

After a while longer on the road, the boys heard a chugging engine coming up behind them. It was a farm tractor pulling a wagon. The man driving the tractor stopped and shouted over his engine, but Friedhelm couldn't understand what he was saying.

"What?" Friedhelm yelled back.

Then, in uneven German, the man shouted again. "Get. In!" They eagerly threw their sleds and suitcases onto the wagon and found a place where they could stand right behind the driver, holding on to his seat.

He told the boys, as he drove, that he was a prisoner of war from Poland and that he had a wife and two children waiting for him there. Like a number of prisoners of war, he had been assigned to a farm, where he was to replace the farmer who had been drafted into the German military and was serving somewhere in Russia or on the western front in France.

"Were you a soldier?" Friedhelm asked him.

"I was a truck driver! I have no business being in this mess." He shook his head. "Back then, I drove a truck for the Poles, and now I drive a tractor for the Germans. But it's more different than you would think."

They rode in silence for a while. Each time another company of soldiers marched by, they forced the Polish man off the road so they could keep going. Their progress was slow and arduous.

Then, when there were no troops to be seen anywhere on the road, ahead or behind, he stopped the tractor again. "That's it, boys. You walk the rest of the way."

"Where are you going?" Friedhelm asked.

"This is my best chance. I'm going home!" He helped them off the wagon, wished them God's blessing, and drove the tractor east, toward the sunrise, toward Poland, free at last.

They watched him until they couldn't see him anymore and then resumed walking up the road.*

((ı))

The boys weren't the only ones making slow progress. The buses that had left Neustettin the night before stopped and started through the whole trip. Again and again, they pulled off the road to wait while the military passed in the opposite direction. This little country road had never seen so many traffic jams. When the caravan finally arrived in the next village, the drivers parked on the west side of a church and were told by the commander of the NSKK troop from Neustettin to go no farther.

"What's happening?" Brunhild asked her mother. "Why did we stop?"

Gertrud shook her head, and they stepped off the bus.

Ernst-August's unit, the NSKK, was also in the village, but they were now under orders to return to Neustettin. The attack, which German intelligence had predicted would begin overnight, had not come. Instead, the Russian tanks had taken the opportunity to regroup farther to the east. Their town was safe, at least for the time being, and the Germans were using the opportunity to reinforce the town and rethink their strategy.

While the bus drivers conferred with the leaders of the NSKK, Gertrud began working on a strategy of her own. She knew that this delay was her best chance to reunite her family. In the chaos of the night before, she had not only lost track of Friedhelm, she also had no idea about the safety of Gisela. And she had no desire to see her oldest son, a boy of fourteen, ride back to Neustettin to face the oncoming Russian tanks.

From the bus she saw Ernst-August standing with the two or three other junior members of the NSKK, joking and roughhousing. Gertrud got off the bus and told Brunhild to watch their luggage. She would be back soon. She crossed the street into the churchyard. "Bubi!" she called, waving her arms in the air.

His new friends started cajoling him, waving their arms around and teasing, "Bubi! Your mommy wants you, Bubi!" None of them had their mothers around, watching or nagging them. Ernst-August play-punched one of them, to try to regain some face, but then he came running over to her.

"Yes, Mother?"

She led him behind the church, away from the soldiers and the NSKK. "Your brother is missing."

"Missing?"

"The bus left him in Neustettin. We need to go back. We need to find him."

Ernst-August saw the distress she was in and took a moment before answering. "I can't leave. I have orders."

She shook her head. "No, your military career is over. You're coming with us." She opened her suitcase and handed him some of his civilian clothes. "Take off that uniform and put these on. We're going."

He shifted uneasily from one leg to the other but didn't move any closer, and he didn't reach out for the offered clothes.

"That would be desertion," he said.

Gertrud looked at her boy, standing apart from her in his sharp uniform. His boots and pant legs were speckled with dirt that had splashed up from his beloved motorcycle. Around the corner of the church, by the road, his new friends from the NSKK were laughing at something. In the midst of this war and this evacuation, these boys were having a grand old time. A brave, heroic, romantic, exciting time. Their jobs, she realized, made them feel important, and they loved that feeling.

She had already lost one of her sons tonight, and now she saw that she was losing another.

"Bubi, he's your brother. We can't leave him." When he didn't move, she pleaded. "Please?"

She hated that she had started crying, but she couldn't stop it.

He stood stoic. "I can't do what you are asking, Mother. I should get back."

"Bubi!" she called one more time as he began walking away. Then, "Ernst-August."

He stopped and looked back at her, and she offered him the clothes one more time. "If you won't put them on, please just take them. In case you need them later."

He stood for another moment, considering. Then he took the clothes from her and stuffed them deep into his rucksack. "I should get back," he repeated and jogged back around the building to return to his unit.

Gertrud sat down in the snow of the churchyard, and this time she didn't try to stop the crying. She just let it come.

"Mama!"

Brunhild was calling her.

"It's Friedhelm! Friedhelm is here!"

And there he was, next to his sister, still tugging the sled and suitcase behind him.

"How did you find us?" she said, clutching him to her. "How did you know to come?"

"Simple," Friedhelm said, wondering what all the fuss was about. He patted his mother gently on the back as she hugged him. "I knew the direction the buses were going, so that's the direction I walked in. I figured I'd find you sooner or later. I had to." He did not tell her how scared he had been.

Gertrud wiped her tears and held her youngest son close, a silent prayer of gratitude on her lips.

CHAPTER 17

CROSSING INTO GERMANY: JANUARY 1945

THE JOB FAMILY watched from the back of the military truck as it crossed what had, until the war, been the German border with Poland. Ludwig woke Eduard and Georg, one sleeping on each of his shoulders. "Look," he said, showing them. "We're in Germany."

Soon all the children were climbing to the back of the truck to get a better look. They had grown up speaking the German language, thinking of themselves as German people, and now they were all full-fledged German citizens—but they had never before been to Germany. The fear and distress they had felt at being so suddenly displaced from their home during yesterday's quick evacuation were replaced, at least a little, by the thrill of this new adventure.

"We're in Germany!"

Ludwig, who had spent so much time over recent years crossing back and forth between Poland and Germany, smiled at his children's exuberance. They eagerly scanned the landscape, looking to point out any difference they could find between what they saw here in Germany and what they had seen in their Polish homeland. Whenever they spotted a sign along the road, they would race to read it aloud in German.

But while his children were staring excitedly ahead into Germany, Ludwig gazed wistfully back toward Poland. Poland had always been his home, and despite the conflicting loyalties introduced during the war, he was sad to leave it. He didn't know when—or if—he would return. But he knew that whether the Soviets occupied the country or it was somehow returned to the Poles, the place would offer no haven to a Volksdeutscher like himself, at least not any time soon.

He also didn't know what place he and his family would next be able to call home. They were thoroughly displaced.

From the other side of the truck bed, Eveline caught Ludwig staring backward. She knew exactly what he was thinking, because she was thinking the same thing. It felt strange to be leaving her homeland on her birthday. Her own history was so completely intertwined with the history of Poland, a history full of exploitation and profound suffering. For a moment her mind went back to her days at the University of Warsaw, where her student ID had shown the Polish version of her family name, Wittówna, rather than the German Witt. She sighed sadly as their home country receded from view and reached for Ludwig's hand.

Before long their caravan of trucks pulled into a town and stopped at the railroad station. There, the German officer who had rescued the Jobs from Kalisz negotiated with an administrator at the train station and secured passage for the family on the first train headed west.

"Good luck," he called to the family after they'd said their goodbyes and removed their luggage from the truck bed.

"You too," Ludwig said as he shook the man's hand. By now it was clear to all of them, though no one was saying it out loud, that the end of the war was near and that Germany would not be on the winning side. No one knew what destiny would bring them in the coming days. These soldiers were retreating and regrouping, but it was inevitable that they would face the Russian army before long.

Ludwig grabbed the extra Philips radio they had in their luggage and offered it to the officer. "Maybe this will help somehow to keep you out of trouble."

The soldier took the radio gratefully. "Thank you," he said.

The family watched as the trucks drove off, and then they gathered their bags and boarded the train.

It wasn't a normal passenger train, but rather a freight train made up of two windowless boxcars behind a long series of flat cars, all of them covered in several inches of snow. The boxcars were already crammed full of refugees taking shelter from the cold, but the flat cars were almost completely vacant. Ludwig and his family cleared the snow from one of the flat cars and settled in as best they could for the trip. Whenever the train was not moving, Ludwig played games with the children to keep them running, jumping, and active at all times to avoid getting too cold, and when they grew tired, they bundled under the feather quilts and wool blankets Eveline had wisely packed.

The train made slow progress westward. Each time it came upon a military train, the freight train would pull onto a side track to cede the right of way and wait until the other train had passed. Then it would continue on its way.

When the train crawled through the German villages and towns, the children ran around the flat car with even more excitement, shouting out the names on the signs and waving at passersby. Their enthusiasm grew stronger as the train went deeper into the Fatherland. Everything they had seen and learned during their years in school was suddenly becoming real before their eyes.

"It's like coming home," Eduard told his father.

I hope so, Ludwig thought. *We'll see.*

When darkness fell the train made another stop, and a group of nurses walked alongside the flat cars, asking all mothers and children to move into one of the boxcars to protect themselves from the severe cold.

"Come on," Ludwig told the children. "Time to go inside." He could see that the frigid air was already taking a toll on the children. They were shivering and blue-lipped and having trouble staying awake.

"We don't want to leave you, Daddy!" Elizabeth started crying.

"You'll sleep in the toasty warm boxcar, and then you'll see me in the morning."

Ludwig said good night to each of them and then wrapped himself up in the wool blankets while Eveline and Emma took the children inside.

The boxcar had been converted, somewhat, to be a bit more hospitable. A sort of loft created a second floor of bunk beds to fit more people inside, and there was a makeshift *Kanonenofen*, a small iron stove with a chimney running out the roof of the boxcar and a blazing fire inside, so the car was cozy and warm despite the subzero air outside.

But it wasn't quiet. Soon after the Jobs entered the boxcar, a woman on the lower bunk started crying out in pain . . . and went into labor. Eveline and many of the other women on the train volunteered to be impromptu midwives, boiling water on the Kanonenofen, bundling the woman in blankets, and trying to coach and comfort her through her pain throughout the entire night while the children tried to sleep.

When the baby was born, the boxcar erupted in cheers, and the new mother wept with joy and relief and clutched her new daughter close to her chest. "Wanda," she said. "I'm going to call her Wanda." *Wanderer.*

When the morning sun started to shine through the slats in the boxcar, the children tugged at Eveline and Emma and asked if they could go back outside to be with their father.

"Not yet," she told them. "We have to wait until the train comes to a stop."

They were restless to get back outside and take another look at the countryside, and every time the train paused on its journey, they scrambled to collect their things and get closer to the door. But then the train would lurch forward again before the children were able to get out of the boxcar.

"We will wait," Eveline told them, "until we come to a full stop, in a town." In truth, she was even more eager to get out of the boxcar than they were. She was worried about Ludwig. The night had been terribly cold, and she needed to know that he was all right.

Finally, the train stopped at a station. As soon as the boxcar doors opened, the Job children clambered to freedom and ran along the tracks toward the front of the train until they found the flat car where Ludwig and some other men had spent the night.

"Daddy!"

Ludwig hugged his children and tickled their faces with the stubble on his unshaven face. Eveline and Emma followed the children up onto the car. They were reunited just as the train again started rolling forward.

But something was wrong. As the train pulled away from the station, the people on the flatcar saw that the two boxcars had been left behind. Somehow, they had become decoupled from the rest of the train while they were in the station.

The train picked up speed on its way out of town.

The man next to Ludwig stood up, slow to understand what was happening, and then screamed, "No!" His wife and children were still in the boxcars, and they were getting farther away with each passing moment. But the train was already galloping down the rails, away from town, much too fast for him to jump off safely. He nearly jumped anyway, and would have if Ludwig and some other men hadn't grabbed onto him. He fought against them for a few moments and then fell into their arms, shouting and crying, while Eveline held her own children close to her and said a silent prayer for the man.

As the sun slowly heated up the cold train car, Ludwig and Eveline began discussing their options. A return to their native Poland was out of the question. Ludwig knew that he was expected to return to Philips, but under the circumstances he had no inclination to go to Krems or Porta Westfalica until he could be assured of his family's safety.

He also knew that the corporation offered them the promise of some safety and security in what were otherwise very uncertain times. Thanks to Philips, the Job family had opportunities that, Ludwig knew, few people on this train of refugees had.

He thought about how he had even come to work for the company. His father-in-law had recommended him for the position. And how had he first met his father-in-law? The church. Ludwig had thought often lately about God's providence and the shelters it had provided for his family, and he was deeply, unspeakably grateful.

They considered aiming for Hamburg, where Philips was headquartered. It would be straightforward enough for Ludwig to transfer to a position in the lab there. But it was less clear whether this would be a safe option for the family. Hamburg was being subjected to severe Allied bombing, with no end in sight. Whole sections of the city had been reduced to ruin, and Ludwig had no desire to add his children to the growing number of civilian casualties there.

Eveline's mother, sister, and in-laws had fled their own homes the previous year and had just relocated again, to a small town called Bärwalde. Wouldn't it make sense for Ludwig and Eveline to take their children, along with Emma and her son, to the same town? It wasn't likely that Ludwig would be able to stay with them very long—he would have to return to Philips—but at least this congregation of families would have one another for safety and mutual support.

It was a good plan.

At the first opportunity, when they came to a larger town, the Jobs disembarked from their freight train and bought tickets on a crowded passenger train to the city of Frankfurt on the Oder. From there, they would be able to transfer to another line that would take them down the Oder River toward Küstrin and toward Eveline's family in the town of Bärwalde.

"We're not going with you," Emma told them once they'd settled onto the Frankfurt-bound train. "This train is going on to Berlin, and my son and I are staying on."

"You can't do that." Eveline argued. "We need to stay together!"

"We need to be safe!" Emma countered. "And if Berlin isn't safe, then nowhere is."

At the time, she could not have known that the Russian army would reach Berlin ahead of the western Allies. How she would have liked to discuss her options with her husband, Richard Job. Emma hadn't heard from him since Christmas, when he had written about the fierce battles on the eastern front in which he and his company were engaged. His letter had mentioned the loss of many comrades to the bullets of the enemy. But what she would not learn until much later was that Richard was no longer among the living, that the battlefield had demanded his life some eight days before they had left Kalisz. She would not find out this devastating news for months.

The two women fought the whole way to Frankfurt, but Emma couldn't be persuaded, and eventually Eveline conceded that it wasn't her decision to make. "Please send word where we can find you once you're settled."

They traded hugs, and the Job family disembarked and waited on the platform to wave at Emma and her son as the train pulled out of the station toward Berlin. Then they boarded their own train to Bärwalde. Emma did make it to Berlin and her new home. After the end of the war, it took a long time before she obtained Eveline's address and the two started corresponding with each other.

Eveline's mother, Eugenia, and her sister Frieda were grateful to see the Jobs arrive safely, and they gave them a fantastically warm welcome. Frieda knew of an apartment nearby that had been recently vacated by refugees moving farther west, and the town officials said it would be fine for the Jobs to move in.

Eugenia was staying with Frieda and Frieda's three daughters. The Jobs had only just arrived in town, and they were already surrounded by relatives and loved ones. Eveline was still worried about Emma, regretting that she wasn't there too. "She should be here with us," she told Ludwig. "Safe with her family."

"She did what she felt was right," he replied.

Ludwig walked with his children along winding cobblestone streets. They were lined with gaslights and shops labeled in artisanal, hand-painted signs, and his children were still excitedly reading them aloud. *"Fleischer!"* Butcher. *"Bäcker!"* Baker.

His adventurous trip to Kalisz to rescue his family had been a success. He would remain with them for another week, to make sure they had everything they needed, and then, according to the arrangement he had made with Philips, he would relocate to Hamburg and join their research team there.

The war would be over soon—it had to be—and they had weathered it safely.

He marveled again how a faithful God had delivered them all so quickly out of the unknown and into shelter and sanctuary.

This truly is a miracle, Ludwig thought to himself.

CHAPTER 18

KOLBERG: FEBRUARY 1945

THE RUSSIANS HELD OFF on their attack on Neustettin, and the buses that had ferried the civilians out of harm's way were ordered to return to town.

Gertrud had other ideas. Her oldest son, Ernst-August, had ridden off with his unit, back into Neustettin, and she hadn't been able to stop him. She realized that his fate was now out of her control. But she decided then and there that she must do everything in her power to protect the two children she still had at hand, Friedhelm and Brunhild, and also try to learn whatever she could about the whereabouts of Gisela.

She made up her mind not to return home. It wasn't possible to keep her family safe there, she thought, with the Red army poised to invade at any moment. Instead, their best option would be to make their way north to the Baltic coast, to her parents' hometown of Kolberg. Luckily, Gertrud knew the area well, and she knew how to navigate the small country roads that connected the various villages along the way.

But unfortunately for the three of them, the bus had left them in a small village with no train line going north toward the Baltic Sea. The only way for them to get to Kolberg would be to set out walking. They headed for Belgard, a town they had visited periodically on account of its Baptist church—the same church where Gisela had been baptized the previous year.

Belgard also had good rail line connections. If they could get there, they might be able to catch a train the rest of the way to Kolberg.

Gertrud and Friedhelm loaded their luggage onto Friedhelm's sled and tied it down so it wouldn't come loose during their long trek. Then they set off. They walked six hours, nearly without a break, Gertrud and Friedhelm taking turns tugging at the sled and six-year-old Brunhild occasionally riding on it to rest her feet. They chose side roads to stay out of the way of military traffic, and when the sun got low in the sky, they knocked on the door of a farmhouse, hoping they could plead with the owner to let them spend the night in the empty barn.

The kindly old farmer looked at this woman and her two children, who had been walking in the cold all day and had worn their hands and feet through with blisters, and told them that under no circumstances could they stay in his barn. Instead, he invited them to stay in his living room. He cooked them a hot meal of soup and gave them each a blanket to use in the night. The next morning, he brewed Gertrud a cup of grain coffee and offered them slices of bread with real jam.

They had another long day of walking ahead of them, but the day was safe and uneventful. They dragged their tired feet into the town of Belgard late that afternoon and headed straight to the train station.

"We need three tickets to Kolberg," Gertrud said at the ticket counter.

"No trains to Kolberg today," the man replied.

"Tomorrow, then," Gertrud acquiesced.

"No trains tomorrow," the man told her.

Her exhaustion started to get the better of her. She was losing her patience. "Are there no trains to Kolberg?"

The man shook his head and pointed to the many wounded soldiers who were lined up at the far end of the station. "The only train going to Kolberg is a hospital train for the war wounded. It leaves later tonight."

Gertrud thanked the man now that he had finally given her some useful information. She marched over to the officer in charge of the hospital train and beseeched him to allow them passage on his train. He looked ready to refuse her, but when he saw the two children, stalwartly heaving heavy bags that were nearly their own size, he changed his mind. “I can’t offer you seats,” he warned her.

“We don’t need seats,” Gertrud assured him. “You won’t even know we are there.” With that the officer let them climb onto the train, asking them to remain standing in the passageway and not enter the area of the car that offered compartments and beds for the wounded soldiers. There was room for the three and for their luggage and the sled. And before the night was out, they were on their way to Kolberg.

August Rattunde, Gertrud’s father, was grateful to see them. “Thank God you made it out safely,” August said when they arrived. “We heard the Russians were approaching Neustettin, and we feared the worst.” Then he confided to her, “Your mother is very sick, in bed with pneumonia. War or no war, I’m glad you’re here. She’ll be happy to see you.”

Then August turned to greet his grandson. “Friedhelm, you must have gotten quite strong since I saw you last if you’ve been able to pull that sled all across Pomerania. You’re like a little Hercules, carrying so many bags. Let me help you with those.”

August winked at him, and for the first time since the start of their journey, Friedhelm thought of the strange lady who had stayed at their house several years ago, trekking across the country with her suitcases, looking for refuge from the war. He remembered how his grandfather had been there when the lady moved into their house and how they had helped her carry her bags and then unpack them so she would feel at home. The lady had long since moved on to another town, to reunite with her family—exactly as Friedhelm was doing now.

August scooped up his granddaughter. “And you, Brunhild! I imagine you’ve been riding in that sled like a little princess!” He tickled her, and she ran giggling and squealing into the house, as if life were normal and there weren't a war raging outside.

August was right: Pauline was delirious with fever, but when she saw her eldest daughter and grandchildren, her eyes lit up. "We were so worried," she murmured, squeezing Gertrud's hand. "We heard the reports on the radio and thought you might not make it out of Neustettin alive." Gertrud stroked her mother's soft skin and thought how good it was to see her parents. She wondered why it so often took such extreme circumstances for people to appreciate what they have.

Her sister Lotte and Lotte's husband, Bruno, had a furnished apartment in the city center of Kolberg, but Bruno had been drafted and sent to the Eastern Front, and Lotte had fled west with her daughter, leaving the apartment empty. It was a twenty-minute walk from August and Pauline's home. The Radandts moved in that very night and unpacked their things.

There they settled back into a normal life, or at least as normal as they could hope for under the conditions. Friedhelm and Brunhild had many cousins in nearby Gross-Jestin, the small town where he had been born. Normally, these cousins would have been attending school in Kolberg, but schools had closed in January until further notice—too many people were leaving town. The signs of war and the approaching front lines were everywhere.

Friedhelm gave over his afternoons to exploring the town. He had been here before, and he spent enough time visiting to have a feel for the place—but Kolberg had changed significantly during the intervening months.

This beautiful resort town was known for its white beaches, which during the summer months were covered with roofed wicker chairs. Townspeople and tourists would rent the chairs for the season. A well-maintained park with tall trees separated the beaches from the town itself. The red brick cathedral in the city center reflected Kolberg's old and famous history. Now, each day, new refugees arrived on foot or on horse-drawn wagons, and the narrow city park along the Baltic Sea was filled with an encampment of horses and wagons and people. These refugee families built little fires to cook their meals while they waited for an opportunity to flee further west. With the Russians moving ever closer and threatening to cut off any escape route parallel to the sea, the fate of these refugees became more desperate by the day.

More and more military units arrived daily for the inevitable battle to come. The army installed a battery of heavy guns in the park, enormous cannons that smelled of oil and cordite and had their paint peeling off from so much repeated use. The guns were surrounded with piled sandbags and stockpiles of artillery shells and guarded by unshaven soldiers who seemed always to be smoking cigarettes despite the obvious danger of doing so in close proximity to so many explosives. They were grim, hardened men, seasoned on the Eastern Front. They had seen terrible things and had already escaped death more times than they'd thought possible.

Their orders were clear.

The city of Kolberg had, through its long history, been the birthplace of many courageous and victorious military leaders, including the fearless naval commander Joachim Nettelbeck. He became known as the defender of Kolberg when in 1806 he urged the city not to capitulate before Napoleon Bonaparte. The following year, he was victorious in leading the battle for freedom against the French. The Nazi propaganda ministry had been drawing on the city's legends to inspire the German people to take a heroic stand against the incoming Russians. Hitler had commanded the army to defend Kolberg to the last man. There could be no surrender.

But the soldiers in charge of the city's defense looked exhausted and afraid. By now they had seen enough with their own eyes that propaganda held little sway over them. Orders were orders, and desertion wasn't a possibility. But no one could order them to hope.

Friedhelm walked with his sister through Kolberg and watched as the city entrenched itself for battle. He had never seen such big guns before, and certainly not so close up. He asked a soldier if he could touch one of them, and the soldier just shrugged. "Be careful not to set anything off. We don't want to start the battle any sooner than we have to."

The metal of the cannon was cold, so cold that Friedhelm worried his fingers might stick to it. But he knew it wouldn't stay like that much longer. Whenever the guns started firing, they would quickly become too hot to touch.

Friedhelm described everything he saw in a letter he wrote to his brother. He addressed the letter to the Rottenführer Ernst-August Radandt and sent it to the NSKK in Neustettin, though by now there was no way to know if his brother or his unit were still there. He wondered if Ernst-August had seen artillery guns as big as these. He wondered if he had seen any Russians.

While Friedhelm was at his grandparents' house, he helped to care for his sick grandmother. He worked in the kitchen with his mother and his grandfather to cook broth for her, since it was the only food she could get down her sore throat. He would fetch blankets for her when she was cold and cool, wet towels to help break her fever when she was hot. When the fever was strongest, she would toss and moan and didn't always seem to know where she was, and when he touched her and felt how hot her skin was, he thought again of those artillery guns in the park. But when her fever broke, she came back to her family, lucid and funny and kind. She listened to their stories and even told a few of her own. When the fever broke, she was their grandmother again.

Living in Uncle Bruno and Aunt Lotte's apartment, they were careful to leave things more or less as they'd found them and not to disrupt their aunt's and uncle's personal belongings. Friedhelm's mother would say, "Aunt Lotte will need to be able to find everything when she gets back" or "What will Uncle Bruno say if he sees that you left his room like that?"

But Friedhelm didn't know if Uncle Bruno or Aunt Lotte were coming back. If they were, it certainly wouldn't be soon.

And if Uncle Bruno and Aunt Lotte weren't coming back to their apartment, what did that mean for the Radandts' own house in Neustettin? Would they ever see it again? He'd only been gone a few weeks, but he already imagined that he would probably never go back. They'd left chickens in the coop, he remembered. *What has happened to our chickens?* he wondered. *Did the neighbors come and rescue them?*

He looked out the window. It was only a little after dawn, and most of the town was still dead quiet, but he saw a lone truck driving through the street, zigzagging side to side, then stopping. When it stopped, men got out, ran toward one of the apartment buildings, and then returned from the building carrying a large bundle. They threw the bundle into the truck and then drove on, again stopping at another building and doing the same thing.

With horror, Friedhelm realized the bundles were corpses. Overnight, people on this city block had died, and these soldiers were retrieving the bodies.

What had happened?

As if in answer to his question, Friedhelm heard the distant rattle of machine gun fire.

All at once, Friedhelm's whole family seemed to be awake. His mother was running from room to room, collecting their things, and Brunhild stood at a sink, turning the faucet and watching a slow trickle of water finally peter out. "Why isn't there any water, Mommy?"

Gertrud didn't answer. "Brunhild, put on your sweater and your shoes."

Brunhild still looked confused. "Friedhelm, why isn't there any water?"

Somehow, instinctively, he knew the answer to her question. He couldn't explain how he knew, but he did.

"Do what Mother told you, Brunhild. Put on your sweater and your shoes. We're going outside, and it's cold." He too pulled on a sweater and began lacing up his boots. "Hurry."

"Why? Why are we going outside?"

He helped her tie her shoes and wrapped a scarf around her neck.

"Ready?" his mother asked him.

He nodded.

The Russians had reached the waterworks.

The siege of Kolberg had begun.

CHAPTER 19

HAMBURG: FEBRUARY 1945

THE STORY WAS becoming all too common for the Job family. They would arrive somewhere new, settle into what they hoped would be a sanctuary where they could wait out the end of the war, and then, shortly after, they would wind up fleeing in a rush to avoid the still oncoming Russians.

In all, the Jobs spent one peaceful week in the town of Bärwalde with Eveline's mother and her in-laws, the Rosners, before a radio news announcement alerted them that the Russian Red Army was advancing much farther and much faster than anyone had expected. The German Wehrmacht was offering almost no resistance at all, and the Russians moved toward Berlin with incredible speed, slowing periodically only to regroup and reinforce their supply lines. There seemed to be no plan or force in place to stop them.

The only real barrier that might slow the approach of the Russians was one that was mentioned again and again on the radio these days: the Oder River would delay their advance. They would need to calculate the best strategic routes to march their amassed forces across the limited number of bridges and ferry points, and that would take time.

So the Russians were intending to march forward to the Oder River and then pause before continuing on to Berlin.

But Ludwig's family was on the east side of the river—the Russian side. Judging by the radio report, they would fall under attack from the fearsome Red Army within a day. The Jobs and the Rosners knew they had to leave immediately and continue westward in order to escape.

Ludwig, practiced for years at waking early, rose before dawn to ready his family. The family quickly packed up the apartment that had been their temporary home and then walked to meet the Rosners. The plan was for all of them to catch the 7:00 a.m. train west out of Bärwalde. From there, Ludwig and his family would try to make their way on to Hamburg, and the Rosners would head to Wuppertal.

First, though, they needed to get a safe distance from the front line.

But the Rosners were having trouble gathering up all their things. They had moved more things with them when they came to Bärwalde than the Jobs had brought, some considerable investments, and they struggled to decide what they could afford to bring and to leave behind.

Ludwig felt it was no time for sentimentality or frugality, and he tried to help them with their decision making. "Friends, it doesn't matter what you bring. It matters that you bring yourselves, so we don't miss the 7:00 a.m. train."

But the Rosners needed more time, and according to the radio reports, the Russians were still hours away.

"You go ahead," Oma Witt told the Jobs. "We will catch the 9:00 a.m. train."

Neither Ludwig nor Eveline worried overly when they boarded their train at 7:00 a.m. and pulled out of town. They had every reason to believe that the rest of their family would safely escape on the next train out of Bärwalde.

They didn't learn until later that there were no other trains out of Bärwalde—that the rail lines shut down just after they left, that the Russian tanks arrived shortly after, and that the Rosners were forced into their own strange and frightening adventure during the months that followed. When little Elizabeth asked, "Where's Oma?" Eveline told her, truthfully to the best of her knowledge, that Oma would be on the next train.

Meanwhile, Ludwig and Eveline pondered whether their plan to go to Hamburg was best for their family. But they were running out of options. One by one, all the safe havens they'd selected for themselves had been overrun, and Ludwig was tired from so much fleeing. He knew Hamburg and had come to love it, and he knew people there who could help them. The city was still under notoriously severe Allied bombing, but he couldn't think of any other, more advisable option, a place where they could stay together as a family during these last few days or weeks of the war. *Surely, the war has to end soon* was the prayer that gave him confidence.

Once they arrived in Stettin, Ludwig felt at home. He had changed trains here before. He led the family to the right platform, and they nestled in among the crowd of other refugees and waited.

But finding a train that was actually going to Hamburg proved to be harder than he had imagined. Each time a train pulled into the station, Ludwig would push his way through the crush of people to ask one of the conductors, "Is this train going to Hamburg?" The conductor would usually tell him the train's intended destination and would sometimes even offer him the whole list of towns the train would pass through en route. But no one said Hamburg. And none of the people working on any of the trains seemed too sure about their final destination either. The trains were constantly being diverted and rerouted to avoid the Russians in the east and south and the Allied bombing from the west.

The Jobs watched trains pull into the station in Stettin already filled with refugees and then depart even more full. But they themselves could not find a train.

They stood on the platform normally used for trains going to Hamburg, and they watched, and they waited.

Finally, a train pulled up to their platform. Like the trains before it, this one was brimming with refugees. But Ludwig saw that the last car of the train was empty except for a few people, and its doors were closed and locked.

"What about that car?" he asked the conductor, but the man shook his head.

"That car is reserved."

The crowd of refugees at the station gathered around the empty car, trying to get a glimpse inside, though by now the few people inside the car had drawn the window blinds shut. Finally, the crowd drew the attention of the Nursing Corps, assigned to the station to help manage the throng of displaced people.

"What's going on here?" the head nurse asked the man guarding the door. "Open the door."

"Sorry, ma'am," he explained. "This car has been requisitioned by the government. It's for the exclusive use of Nazi officers."

She pulled herself to her full height and said, brusquely, "I'll have you know I *am* a Nazi officer." It was true; the Nursing Corps was an arm of the government, and the head nurse held an officer's rank. "Now open this door."

The conductor sheepishly unlocked the train car, and the Nazi officers inside immediately stood up, shouting, "No refugees in here!"

But the head nurse wouldn't relent. "Shame on you, sitting in here, smoking and drinking while these families wait helplessly for a train. There are women and children here! Who do you think you work for, if not the people of Germany?"

The abashed officers looked at one another and then acquiesced. "I suppose we can make an exception," one of them said, and they all moved toward the back of the car to make space for the refugees.

"Well don't just walk away," the nurse barked at them. "Help them with their luggage!"

That was enough for Ludwig and his family. They boarded the car, picked their seats, and relaxed into them as the train began to roll out of the station. Whether the train was bound for Berlin or would go on to Hamburg, no one knew. The train was headed west, and that was what mattered.

As they rounded a bend, Eduard looked out the window at the back of the train. "Father, look!" Behind all the passenger cars were a series of freight cars, and on one of them, Eduard had spied the luggage and bedding the Jobs had loaded on board their prior train in Bärwalde. Even during the chaos of war, the German rail service had managed to deliver their luggage to the right platform.

The train passed through the West Pomeranian territory and on into the province of Mecklenburg. The engineer had to change routes again and again to avoid stations that had been hit by bombs and tracks that had been rendered impassable. Occasionally the train stopped on open tracks and sat idle, waiting for orders before daring to move on.

Still, as station after station was announced, Ludwig realized that they were moving farther and farther west, away from the front line.

Before long, a conductor came through the passenger car to announce that their train would be going on to Lübeck. Ludwig had never been to Lübeck—it was a beautiful medieval city on the Baltic Sea—but he knew his geography well enough to know that it was only about an hour north of Hamburg. Going to Lübeck was the best thing that could happen to them.

In Lübeck, signs of war were everywhere. The city, once known for its red-brick Gothic architecture, had been bombed terribly. Many of those red-brick Gothic churches and historic buildings lay in ruins. But at the station, the trains came and went on schedule, arriving and departing from their usual platforms as if there weren't a war at all. All the Jobs needed to do to continue on to their destination was cross over to another platform and pick up a routine transfer.

By evening, they were in Hamburg.

They walked through the huge entrance hall of the city's old railroad station, the Hauptbahnhof, which Ludwig had passed through several times while doing work for Philips. He knew his way around perfectly. He looked instinctively at the clock tower—though Allied bombs had ruined it more than a year ago—and realized that today was the last day of January. They had traveled all the way from the Oder River in eastern Germany to Hamburg in just one long day. A week ago, they had been moving into an apartment in Bärwalde near Eveline's family. Two weeks ago, they had been safely ensconced in Kalisz, going on about their lives. Five weeks ago, they had been unwrapping Christmas presents.

What a terrible month they'd had. And what a miraculous one too.

They weren't safe here in Hamburg, either—at least not yet. The signs of war were everywhere. Cold wind whipped through the station, because the glass dome above the Hauptbahnhof and all of the station's glass windows had been shattered. Pieces of broken glass were scattered all over the tracks.

A corps of nurses was assigned to the Hauptbahnhof to help identify and sort the incoming refugees, and they found the Jobs right away. The nurses brought the family a meal of hot soup while Ludwig found a pay phone to contact his people at Philips, to let them know he and his family had arrived safely. While he waited for the operators to connect the call, he looked out the window and noticed that he could see the silhouette of the main Philips administrative building from where he stood. It was only a block away.

Ludwig stepped outside the main entrance of the Hauptbahnhof where he had been told to expect a small, covered truck with Philips displayed in large letters. Traffic was light, and Ludwig readily recognized the truck as it drove up. He wasn't sure whether he had met this particular Philips administrator on one of his earlier trips to Hamburg. Acquainted or not, seeing the administrator felt like coming home.

"It's really good to see you and to have you take us to a place we can call home, at least for now. We are thankful to have made it," Ludwig, with a brimming smile, greeted the man.

"Home? The bombs raining down on the city have destroyed way too many buildings, depriving countless Hamburg residents of their apartments. There is no housing for them. Many of our own people have been forced to leave the city," came the reply.

Ludwig wondered out loud whether he had expected too much. "What about Philips employees who have lost their housing to bombs and fires?"

"We do our best. But it's not only about Hamburg residents. It's also refugees like yourselves coming to the city from the east. This war needs to end."

The firm had arranged to put the family in a vacant school in the Hamburg-Eimsbüttel district. All schools in Hamburg were closed on account of the relentless, ongoing bombing, and this one had been reclaimed and converted into temporary refugee housing. Under the circumstances, this was the best they could do.

The family was assigned to an empty classroom and told they would have it all to themselves. The desks had been removed, and in their place were military cots and wool blankets for sleeping. The closest bathroom was down the hall, but the family was delighted to discover that the classroom had been a science lab of some sort and had sinks with running water.

"Maybe it's not quite the level of comfort you're used to," the Philips official apologized.

"Believe me," Eveline assured him, "this will do."

The administrator also gave them a map, and he drew out explicit directions to the nearest bomb shelter. "Learn more than one way to get there. And learn to get there fast. You will need it."

Then, as he left them to settle in, he said one more thing:

"Welcome to Hamburg."

CHAPTER 20

RITTERGUT DOLGEN: FEBRUARY–MARCH 1945

UNDER NORMAL CIRCUMSTANCES, Gisela Radandt loved all the space at Rittergut Dolgen, the Pomeranian farming estate where she was employed as a nanny to the two Schütze girls. The sprawling fields and rolling dirt roads that separated the main house from the barns and other buildings allowed her many wonderful opportunities to enjoy the countryside while she attended to her day's tasks. In summertime she would walk through the country air with the children and take the opportunity to educate and entertain them. They would often mimic the sounds of the different animals they saw, the ducks and geese and the horses and cows, or practice their numbers by counting clouds in the sky.

And in winter, Gisela and the girls would bundle up in warm coats and blankets and ride behind Mr. Schütze in their winter carriage, a big sleigh pulled by two magnificent horses. They would ride all over the spacious property, up the path along Lake Dolgen and back again, while their old white German shepherd, Max, raced behind them, trying to keep up.

At night, when Gisela was alone, the long walks around the estate gave her time to clear her head, to think about the Schützes and about her own family, and to wander the estate much like her father had done when his job took him to estates like this. But that was before she was born, when he met her mother. Sometimes, walking the long roads at Rittergut Dolgen, she would even let herself daydream about her life after her Pflichtjahr and after the war.

Yes, under normal circumstances, she loved the space at Rittergut Dolgen.

But now plans were being made to deal with the reality of war. The Russians were close. The servants in the Schütze household were busy making ready two wagons for travel, filled with food items, clothing, and other supplies so that the Schützes, along with Gisela and others on the estate, would be ready in the event they needed to evacuate in a hurry. Just a couple of days ago, Gisela had received a letter from her mother telling her that they had made it to Kolberg and were waiting to see what next step they might have to take to stay ahead of the Russians. She had shared that information about her family with the Schützes, who expressed fear of a full-blown attack on Kolberg. She wondered about the safety of her mother and siblings.

That was two days ago, and today was no normal day. Today she was running for her life, and the dirt road that stretched from the house to the stable had never seemed so long.

She had been sitting with the Schütze family for an early lunch when she first noticed their silverware rattling gently against the china, vibrating, so it made a jingling, tingling noise.

"That's odd," she said, pointing it out to the rest of the family.

Mr. Schütze asked for everyone to be quiet, and they all watched as the shaking grew stronger. Soon the whole table was rattling, and the vases on the nearby shelves too.

Then he walked to the window.

Across the field, by the entrance to Rittergut Dolgen, a line of tanks was rumbling up the road.

And now Gisela and the Schützes were running. The loaded wagons full of supplies were still stowed in the barn. The tanks were coming upon them so fast there was no time for them to make it all the way to the stables where the horses were harnessed and back to the barn to hitch the horses to the wagons.

So the adults gathered up the children as quickly as they could, with nothing but the clothes they'd been wearing inside the heated mansion, and they ran out the back door, through the garden, and across the space of Rittergut Dolgen.

"What about Max?" Mrs. Schütze asked before they left the yard. "We can't leave him."

Max, the German shepherd, was a gentle beast with stark white fur who was so big he sometimes reminded Gisela of a polar bear. He had lived with the family for more than a decade, and they couldn't stand to imagine him falling into the hands of the Russians. Mr. Schütze put a leash on the dog. "Hurry, old boy. You're coming with us."

The snow was thick in the fields, and the family trudged through it slowly. Gisela clung to the hands of the two Schütze children, never letting go, trying to keep them from falling behind. Already they could hear the sounds of the Soviet soldiers stumping through the elegant mansion, barking orders and breaking glass, moving from room to room, looking for the owners of the property.

"What will they do if they find us?" Gisela asked.

Ominously, no one answered.

Mr. Schütze aimed the family toward a line of trees on the north end of the estate. From there, he reasoned, they would be able to hide and assess the situation.

The trouble was, there was too little cover in the snowy field. Until they reached the trees, at least a quarter-mile away, there was nowhere for them to hide. If any of the Russian soldiers came to the back of the house, they would see the Schützes for sure.

And if the soldiers saw them and gave chase, there would be no way to outrun them.

They had heard stories about the invading soldiers and the horrors they were inflicting on civilians as they passed from town to town. They would pillage for supplies and take anything of value—that was to be expected, considering the hardships they had all been suffering during this long war. But it was much, much worse than just that.

The Eastern Front had been a particularly gruesome struggle. By now, every one of these soldiers had seen an uncountable number of brutal injuries and deaths. All of them had lost family and friends, and the experiences of the war had habituated many of them to acts of terrible violence. The Red Army had spent the past four years struggling against a German Wehrmacht that had declared "total war" upon them, intent on exterminating their enemy entirely. The Germans were known to starve their prisoners to death or even slaughter them outright. They had never offered their opponent any mercy, and now the Russians reasoned that they deserved none in return.

The soldiers who pushed through Pomerania toward Berlin were, in their minds, avenging the atrocities that had been committed against their own people for years. It was their way of getting some satisfaction and justice.

Gisela had heard rumors. The advancing Russians had become known as Stalin's "army of rapists." They took whatever they wanted, and whether they let you live afterward was entirely a matter of their whims. Their behavior was condoned throughout their entire chain of command. The leaders of the Red Army hoped that inflicting a thorough campaign of humiliation and fear upon the German people would deter any threat of future invasions of the Soviet Union, and they encouraged their soldiers to be as violent and terrifying as they liked.

And there they were now, pouring out the back door of the Schütze's main house.

Half a dozen Russian soldiers watched from the veranda as the desperate family plodded through the heavy snow. The soldiers laughed to see the family trying to escape. They had already seen it so many times.

One of them took aim with his rifle and fired.

Gisela heard the hiss of the bullet pass by her head before she even heard the report of the gunshot.

Mrs. Schütze stumbled in the snow and started to shake uncontrollably.

"Get up," Gisela told her. "We have to keep going."

"Where?" Mrs. Schütze cried. "There is nowhere to go!"

"The lake."

Gisela pointed at the lake that bordered their property. Though it had been frozen most of the winter, a temporary thaw had turned the upper layer of ice into slush, and there was no way to know how thick or strong the remaining ice was. But the family didn't have a chance of escaping the Russians across the field. The lake offered a shorter and faster route, albeit a more dangerous one.

"I'll go first," Mr. Schütze said. "I'm biggest. If the ice will hold me, then it will hold any of you."

He dashed out onto the frozen surface and tested his footing. It seemed to hold.

The family followed him out onto the frozen lake, doing their best to follow exactly in his footsteps.

"Faster!" Mr. Schütze called to them. He watched as the squad of Russian infantrymen marched across the snowy field, getting closer.

Gisela finally picked up the youngest Schütze child in her arms. They couldn't afford to be slowed by her little legs. She heard the ice groan under her feet, stressed by the added weight of the child, and she stopped in fear, listening for any cracking sound that might indicate the ice was failing.

She had spent enough time outdoors in the Pomeranian winter to know that ice doesn't always give a warning before it breaks. Sometimes it just breaks.

She didn't know where to take her next step. The slush was too uneven; there was no way to guess the state of the ice underneath.

Then she heard the voices of the Russian men behind her, and she steeled her resolve. *It's better to fall through the ice,* she thought to herself, *than to wait here and be captured.* She took a step, and then another, and then walked steadily forward without looking down or backward until she reunited with the rest of the Schütze family at the line of trees along the far side of the lake.

The Russians stood at the opposite bank, watching the fleeing family and stepping their booted feet tentatively onto the frozen slush. They decided it wasn't worth the risk. There would be other families, other estates. They turned around and went back into the manor house.

Gisela and the Schützes were safe—for now.

They tramped through the forest and stayed off main roads, and eventually they found their way to the nearby village of Küdde, still on the German side of the front line. There the local farmers had gathered a caravan of wagons and were preparing to leave, aiming west toward Bad Polzin.

The farmer, chosen to act as the leader of the caravan, was just about to finish his inspection. Were all the wagons in solid condition to make the trip? Were any overloaded? Did every horse look strong and healthy, and was there enough feed for all the animals? That's when he and others in the caravan noticed a group of people and a dog coming toward them, apparently a family, but a family of lost souls, for they were out in the forest without being adequately dressed for the cold weather. Immediately, the leader started walking briskly to meet up with them and find out what had happened.

"Mr. Schütze," he exclaimed when he came closer, "what has brought . . ."

But he interrupted himself, and with deep concern and even fear in his voice, continued: "The Russian tanks are already at your Rittergut?"

"Yes, they are," Mr. Schütze told the group of farmers that by now had come within earshot. "We had to run out the back door and across the lake. There was no time to grab our coats and hats or anything else."

The caravan leader abruptly stopped the conversation. "We must get going. There's no time to waste. Let's make room for the Schütze family so they can flee with us. The Russians could show up any minute."

He spoke to a farmer's wife who had room in her wagon. She happily made space for the Schützes and invited them to join her and her children. The farmers found a spot for Gisela in a separate wagon.

The Schützes were reluctant to leave Gisela alone. They took their responsibility as her Pflichtjahr hosts very seriously, and they had promised her father that they would look out for her as if she were a member of their own family. But she assured them she would be fine in the other wagon. "It's best if you all stay together," she told them.

They almost never stopped, except to give the horses some rest, feed, and water. All movement was in one direction. There was no oncoming traffic. Most wagons had a tent cover so one could sit protected against snow and rain but were open to the front and back. During the caravan's slow trek westward, Gisela would often hop off the wagon she was riding to walk alongside it, particularly on open roads. When the caravan was passing through villages and towns, she made sure she was inside the wagon. The farmer and his wife had asked her to do this in order to lighten the load on the horses, but the long walks also helped to stave off the encroaching panic. Where was she going, and what would become of her? What had happened to her family in Neustettin? Had they made it out safely? How would they ever find each other again?

Walking was also the only way she had to keep warm. Even so, she was beginning to lose sensation in her toes. Walking through the snow had soaked her shoes, and after all these hours, some damage was already done. It would turn to frostbite for sure.

She heard the shrill engine of a motorcycle coming up the road from the back of the caravan. It was someone in the military, weaving in and around the long caravan, trying to get through. But when the motorcycle reached her wagon, the young soldier slowed down and started honking.

She couldn't believe her eyes.

"Ernst-August?"

Her brother's windburned face broke into a huge smile. "I saw the Schützes' white German shepherd. I'd recognize that dog anywhere. There's no other quite like it! Mister Schütze told me I would find you up here. But he also told me it's impossible for the caravan to stop. Can you jump from the wagon to my bike?"

He pulled up as close as he could to the moving wagon, and she balanced a foot on the back of his seat and hopped over. Then they rode to the next village so they could talk until the caravan caught up.

While they rode, they shared their stories of the strange events of the past few days. She told him about her harrowing escape from the Russians, and he told her everything he had seen while delivering messages for the NSKK.

"After we got Mother, Friedhelm, and Brunhild out of Neustettin, I was ordered north to Bublitz." Gisela nodded. The two of them knew the town well enough; their mother had grown up there. "In Bublitz, I made personal acquaintance with the Russian tanks, the T-34s. They rode through the town with lazy infantrymen riding on top. They fired their machine guns at me, but none of them hit me."

"Oh, Bubi," she said. "I can't believe you're a soldier now." He had grown so much since she'd left home half a year ago, and she had never before seen him in his sharp, black uniform. His blond hair was cut short and neatly combed; he seemed confident. "I did receive a letter from Mother, telling me that they are now staying in Aunt Lotte's apartment in Kolberg. But is Kolberg safe? Mr. Schütze fears that the battle for Kolberg will be very fierce."

Gisela started to sob: "I am so worried for them. What will happen to them?"

The refugee caravan caught up to them in the village, and Ernst-August had to be on his way. As Gisela climbed back onto the wagon to which she had been assigned, she called out to her brother. "How will we find you, after this is all over?"

But he didn't hear her over the scream of his motorcycle. She watched as he drove up the road and away.

"How will we find you?" she whispered again to herself, knowing there was no answer anyone could give.

CHAPTER 21

HAMBURG: MARCH 1945

"ELIZABETH, HONEY, I need you to wake up."

Eveline gently shook her daughter from the cot where she slept.

Elizabeth was still groggy, and she looked around the room, disoriented. "What time is it, Mommy? Where are we?"

It was still dark in the converted classroom where the Jobs had been living in Hamburg-Eimsbüttel for the last four weeks. Eveline had gone to some trouble to try to make the room more comfortable for her family, more like a home. She didn't have much to work with. There was the set of cots Philips had provided for them, along with a few thin military blankets that were itchy and did little to keep out the winter cold. Philips had also delivered five bulky metal wardrobes to the classroom, hoping the furniture would provide the Jobs an opportunity to unpack and settle in a bit. "What are we going to do with these?" Ludwig had said to Eveline, exasperated. The fact was, after abandoning their home in Poland and then fleeing every subsequent place where they'd hoped to take refuge, they had very little to unpack. At this point, all their worldly possessions would fit into a single wardrobe and not even fill it up.

But Eveline had thought of another use for the wardrobes. She'd dragged them from where they'd been stacked against the wall and arranged them in the middle of the spacious classroom to divide the room into several smaller spaces—a cozy little maze of cabinets so that parents and children had separate sections to call their own.

She also fashioned curtains out of discarded cloth and covered the classroom's windows, partly to give the family some privacy, but also to keep the light of their candles and lamps from leaking out through the windows into the night.

Night was when the bombers flew over Hamburg, and light leaking from windows made them an easy target.

"You know where we are, Elizabeth," she told her daughter while helping her put on her shoes. "We're in Hamburg. We're going to the bomb shelter."

During their first weeks living in the school, there had been a lull in the Allied air raids, and the family had often been able to sleep through the night. They would wake each morning in their strange new home, gather around one of the classroom's laboratory tables for a simple breakfast, and then, once Ludwig had left for work, the rest of them would go out together to run errands.

It was a challenge to settle into a place that had been so damaged by the war. Eveline found her days were invariably full: she needed to collect new IDs for her family, to show that they were now residents of the city. She needed to secure food-rationing stamps and then use them to shop in the unfamiliar streets. And when there was time, she would stop at the Hauptbahnhof, the train station, in the vague hope that she might find the luggage they had shipped from Bärwalde and that Eduard had spotted at the railroad station in Stettin. How happy she was when toward the end of February the agent finally handed her that big package: feather bedding for all in the family!

Because of the bombing there were no schools in session, and Eveline brought the children along on her expeditions in Hamburg, both as a way to keep them occupied and also to stimulate their minds. There was too little to do inside their classroom home—no games or toys, and no other children staying with them in the converted school building. They all loved going outside and exploring.

But the scenes they encountered once they set foot outside the school were haunting. Whichever direction they went, they found mountains of rubbled brick and stone, whole city blocks and neighborhoods demolished by the bombing, alternating with streets where the houses and buildings were still standing. The children would climb around the heaps of debris only to discover more sprawling, surreal landscapes. Sometimes the wreckage stretched for miles. Occasionally, inexplicably, a single house was left standing, while around it on all sides there was nothing but ruin. These scenes offered a sobering reminder of the contrast between the ravished still living and the unfortunate dead.

We are like that, Eveline realized as she walked through Hamburg. *Our family is like one of the few houses left standing amid the ruins.*

These walks filled her with undeniable fear. The landscape made it obvious to her that no place was safe from the bombing. When the raids started again, there would be little that any of them could do to protect themselves except to pray and trust the grace of God.

Not long after they arrived, the family went in search of the Baptist church in the district where they lived. Now that they were refugees, alone in a new city, they hoped to find friends among like-minded believers so they could begin building a new community for themselves.

The address of the church was on Tresckowstrasse in Hamburg-Eimsbüttel, and they knew from the number that the church had to be somewhere within walking distance of their school building—but the family discovered it was remarkably difficult to find one's way through the ruined city. So many landmarks had been destroyed that it was often difficult to discern which street was which, or whether a certain flattened stretch of city was even a street at all.

Ludwig knew this church. He had attended services there during his prior visits to Hamburg in 1942 and 1943, and he knew he would recognize it once he saw it. But by the time the Jobs managed to navigate to the church's location, they were dismayed to discover the old building was in complete ruins, smashed to bits by the bombs.

"Dad, look at this," Eduard called out. The boy had found a notice nailed to the last standing wall of the church, announcing that the congregation was now meeting each Sunday in the assembly hall of the "Albertinenhaus," the home of one of the three German Baptist orders of deaconesses, only a few minutes away.

"The Albertinenhaus?" Ludwig said, surprised. "My niece Marianne lives in the Albertinenhaus." He knew that if that house were still standing, there was a good chance that his niece would still be there.

The following Sunday, the family made their way to the address of the Albertinenhaus, and Marianne recognized Ludwig right away. Elizabeth couldn't take her eyes off her. There she was, dressed in the long, black habit that all deaconesses who had joined this religious order were required to wear. The white, starched cap covered her head, and heartfelt kindness marked that face. Marianne was amazed and delighted to learn that the Jobs were in Hamburg and eager to hear the details of their escape from Poland—her native land—and of their escape from the Eastern Front. After the service she invited the family to stay for coffee and cake and introduced them to other members of the congregation.

Elizabeth told Marianne the story of how they had fled Kalisz and left her doll behind. "That sounds very frightening," Marianne said to her little cousin. Then she went looking through her own things and pulled a bundle out of her closet. "Elizabeth, maybe you can help me with something."

Turning, she presented Elizabeth with a toy: a small, heart-shaped basket, filled to look like a little bed, where two hand-sewn dolls were sleeping. Each one was the size of her thumb. "I've had these dolls a very long time. But now that I'm an adult, I don't have nearly as much time to take care of them as I would like. Since you're here in Hamburg, I'm hoping that you might be able to take care of them for me."

Elizabeth treasured the two dolls and considered it a solemn responsibility that she care for them. She was always careful, even during the air raids, to bring the two little thumb dolls with her wherever she went.

The rest of the church welcomed them as well. It was exactly as the Jobs had hoped. They had found, only a few short days after arriving in the city, a new community of family and friends, of faith and love.

The bombing started again three weeks after the Jobs arrived in Hamburg. Eveline would never forget the first time she heard the wail of the air raid sirens beckoning them to the nearby shelter, several stories high and made of concrete. The sound filled her with an almost paralyzing dread. She knew she had to gather up her children and flee, but she couldn't move. The panic was too much. She was sure the siren wasn't a call to safety; it was a portent of doom.

She forced herself to move anyway, and she and her family marched quickly through the night toward the shelter, walking among the crowds of people who poured out of the many apartment buildings from all directions and walked briskly, without words and without ceremony, into the building. Only when the doors closed and the people felt safe inside the dimly lit sanctuary did anyone talk, and even then only in whispers, while they waited out the night.

That first night, she held her children as they listened to the sounds of the bombs falling, sometimes at a distance, sometimes quite close, shaking the city, over and over—but then finally relenting. The thundering explosions grew farther away and then quieted altogether. The people in charge of the shelter threw open the heavy doors and let the morning sunlight in, and the people all returned, numbly, to their homes.

Still safe. Still alive.

Before long, the family grew practiced at these late-night evacuations. They had to clear out of the schoolroom very quickly, because once the bombers were over the city, it was too dangerous to run through the streets, exposed to the bombs and everything else—the fires, the rubble, and the chaos of war.

The Jobs learned to keep their shoes and their coats near their beds so they could vacate their schoolroom without delay. They also learned a path to the basement of the school building, for the nights when the bombers arrived too quickly to allow them time to flee. The makeshift bunker wasn't as secure as the official air raid shelter, but it was better than nothing.

The raids grew more frequent, three or more a week. Many nights, the family marched through the streets to climb into the shelter and wait out the attack, and when they came back out, sometimes they would see smoldering rubble where earlier there had been buildings. They would see flames leaping out of broken windows and people running desperately in and out of burning buildings, trying to rescue their loved ones or their precious belongings.

Every night like this, the Jobs would say a prayer of thanks to have survived until another morning, and then they would return to the school to try to get some sleep.

"Come on, let's run!" Eveline told Elizabeth over the piercing blast of the air raid siren as the family filed out into the street toward the shelter and forged their way toward the big shelter doors. Eveline felt a clutch of panic as she heard the sound of the bombers in the sky; they were dangerously close already. She reached for her daughter's right hand and held it with a firm grip, while Elizabeth carried her two dolls in the crook of her left arm, clutching them tightly to her chest. They raced down the street that way until they arrived at the shelter.

The shelter was more crowded than usual tonight. As the Allied bombs leveled more of the city, more and more people had been left without homes, and they wandered into other neighborhoods looking for whatever refuge they could find. The Jobs squeezed into the bomb shelter just as the sound of the squadron overhead reached their ears.

They listened to the terrible thundering of the bombs, closer than usual. No matter how many times the family took shelter from these raids, Eveline thought, it never became routine. It was always frightening.

A nearby explosion elicited a collective gasp from the people huddling in the shelter. Ludwig threw an arm around his wife and pulled her close to him. "We will get through this," he whispered to her, as he did each of these nights.

Finally, after a very long night, the sound of the bombs grew more distant and then stopped altogether, and the families were released to return to their residences.

"When will all this be over?" Eveline asked Ludwig, though none of them knew the answer. They could only hope it would be soon. Word had it that the British and American troops were approaching from the west, and Eveline wished they would arrive quickly, to bring an end to the bombing and to the war.

On the walk home, Elizabeth started crying. "Mommy, I can't find them!" Sometime during the night's raid, Elizabeth's two thumb dolls had fallen out of their basket, and now she was bereft. "Marianne needs me to take care of them."

"I'm sure your cousin Marianne will understand," Eveline told her daughter, but Elizabeth was inconsolable. While Ludwig returned home with the boys, Eveline walked with Elizabeth back toward the bomb shelter, retracing their steps, looking carefully for any trace of the dolls.

They found them on the floor of the shelter, or what was left of them. Hundreds of people had walked across the floor on their way home, and they had unwittingly trampled the little dolls to pieces. They were unrecognizable now—just dirty, torn pieces of cloth—and Eveline tried to hide the sight from her daughter, but Elizabeth saw them before she had a chance.

Her mother picked her up and let her sob into her shoulder.

Before she knew it, and against her wishes, Eveline started crying too. There had been so much loss, and she wanted to shield her children from it. But it was too much. It was everywhere. It was seeping into everything. She couldn't keep them safe.

"I'm sorry," she said while she squeezed her daughter. "I'm so sorry, Elizabeth."

CHAPTER 22

KOLBERG: MARCH 1945

THE RUSSIANS HAD SURROUNDED the city of Kolberg. They had reached the waterworks, six miles inland, the night before and cut off all water to the city, the first step in an effort to get the town and the army defending it to surrender.

Then the fighter planes came. They fired their guns but didn't seem to have targets, or at least not strategic ones. They just flew through the city and strafed the streets with bullets. "Yak-1," Friedhelm said quietly to himself. He was still playing the game he'd played all those years with his brother Ernst-August, trying to identify the fleet of aircraft as they passed overhead—though unlike those other times, now the planes were much closer and easier to recognize.

Unlike those other times, now the pilots might actually shoot at him.

Friedhelm was once again dragging his father's suitcase through the streets. They were headed to his grandparents' house, a solid twenty-minute walk even without luggage, when the planes came. Now, his mother and Brunhild were fifty yards ahead of him, racing toward a concrete bomb shelter next to the train station, hoping for cover from the bullets. But because of the weight of his father's suitcase, Friedhelm lagged behind. He stopped every couple of feet to shift the heavy luggage from his one hand to the other and then limped forward, too unbalanced to run. It was slow going, and he watched as the gap widened between him and the rest of his family.

"Mother?" he called out. She didn't hear. Friedhelm wasn't sure they realized how far back he was.

But she wouldn't want him to drop the suitcase. It was the one he'd gone back for in Neustettin—his father's belongings.

A second fleet of fighter planes was approaching. They were low in the sky and still too far away for Friedhelm to recognize, but they were rapidly getting closer. He tried to pick up his pace. The handle from the suitcase was digging into his fingers, and his arm was shaking uncontrollably from carrying so much weight.

What is in this case? he wondered to himself.

The formation of planes got lower and took aim at the street.

Everywhere around him, people screamed and ran for cover.

"Ilyushin Il-2," Friedhelm mumbled to himself as soon as he recognized them. *The Flying Tanks.* The planes were so close, he could see the faces of the pilots in the cockpits, grinning with determination as they pointed their guns at the scrambling crowds.

They fired.

Friedhelm dropped the suitcase and ran just as the bullets rained down. He heard them ricochet off the streets, saw sparks flash as the metal casings smashed into the stone pavement, smelled the burning powder and the fuel from the planes. And he ran.

Finally unburdened of the weight of the suitcase, he sailed quickly through the street and into the shelter of the railway station.

"That's it!" he insisted when he saw his mother. "I'm not going back for that suitcase! I'm not carrying it anymore!"

And she didn't argue. She nodded, quietly accepting what Friedhelm had said. Never again would she risk her son's life to try to protect her husband's belongings—even if they were the only belongings he had left.

Once the planes were gone from the sky, the family continued its walk to the Rattunde house, this time without the extra case. Their path took them through a park where Friedhelm had fond memories from his visit last summer—but he was horrified to see that one of the trees in the park was now strung with the hanged bodies of six deserters, and nearby, a pit had been dug for use as a mass grave. It was already filling up with the corpses of people who had been killed by the Russian artillery.

When they arrived at the Rattunde house, Friedhelm's grandfather was sitting on the front porch, looking somber. Around him, the windows were smashed and the glass scattered across the living room furniture.

"When the planes came," he said, "she couldn't bear it any longer. It frightened her too much."

"What do you mean?" Friedhelm asked. He didn't understand.

"Your grandmother," he said while picking up his handkerchief to wipe away his tears. "She's with God now."

Oma Rattunde, who had been sick with pneumonia and confined to bed these past weeks, had finally given up her fight and gone to rest. She had died moments before Friedhelm and the others arrived.

The German defenses in Kolberg were dug in, and they had every intention of making the Soviet invasion a costly one. As a result, the Russians had decided not to advance directly into Kolberg. Instead, they would wait outside the city, cutting off its supplies of food and water. They shelled it with bursts of artillery fire and waited for their siege to force the city to surrender.

With the Russians taking a slower approach, Friedhelm and his family were in no immediate danger. But in order to survive, they would need to find water, food, and if possible, some way out of town. And in the midst of their new desperation, a woman they loved had died. It had not been a peaceful death, but it had not been brutal, bloody, or painful either, and for that they were all grateful.

They would honor her as best they could, in spite of the circumstances. They would lay her to rest in something beautiful, something precious.

August Rattunde, a cabinetmaker by trade, went to his woodshop and built a casket for his wife. He and Friedhelm dug a grave in the nearby dunes at the edge of the park, and there the family and some friends gathered to give Pauline a proper funeral. Her son Max was only ten miles away in Gross-Jestin, but the siege made it impossible for him to attend the funeral. In fact, the family had no way even to tell Max that his mother had died.

A brief sermon was delivered by the elder of the local Baptist church, a longtime friend. “May this war be over soon,” he concluded.

“Amen,” they answered.

Friedhelm took his mother’s hand, though her cheeks were dry. She held on to him tightly, taking Brunhild in her other hand, and together they walked away from her mother’s grave. They were sad but strangely grateful, grateful that Pauline Rattunde had gone to be with God and left this tortured world behind. A slight breeze blew, and with it, a whisper of gratitude. They were free to go, they realized, now that Oma Rattunde had passed. They were free to leave this place awash in doom. Pauline’s beloved husband and daughter would not have to disturb or frighten her with their exodus. They could flee swiftly and quickly, with no regrets.

Though the house was only a block from the beach, the water from the Baltic Sea was too salty for them to drink. They couldn’t even use it to brew the Ersatzkaffee. But there were still pockets of snow in the shade, and Friedhelm gathered pots full of it and melted them down in the heat of the house so they would have drinking water. And his grandfather discovered that the seawater could be used to make a few loaves of salty bread.

The shelling and bombing continued, and they knew that, under these circumstances, the safest thing for them to do at night was to sleep in a basement. But the Rattunde house didn't have a cellar, so in the evenings the family would walk to an abandoned house on the same block and sleep in that house's basement until morning.

They slept there every night for a week, until one night they were woken by a sharp jolt—a shell had exploded in the building directly above them. It was too close for comfort. It was time for them to try to get out of Kolberg.

The Russians had the town thoroughly surrounded by land. The only way out was to escape by sea. The family packed up their things and headed to the harbor.

By now they had become almost acclimated to the steady blast of artillery shells exploding in the distance, and they walked cautiously but unhurriedly toward the seaport, in relatively good spirits despite the constant rumble of bombs. There were others, headed in the same direction, tired figures who had a hard time carrying their suitcases and bags. Their faces showed that they had gone without food for days.

Then a loud whistle and a thump stopped them in their tracks. A shell—what the German soldiers called a *Stalinorgel* because it hummed like an organ when it flew through the air—had plunged into the ground less than ten feet in front of them but failed to explode. Friedhelm looked at it. It was sizzling hot and nearly half as big as he was. If it had detonated, it would have killed them for sure.

The crowd of people trying to get out of town by boat that day was so huge that it spilled out of the seaport and into the nearby park. Many of the refugees had set up camps and were huddled around their wagons and their smoking fires. There were a number of dead horses among them, though whether they had starved to death or been killed for food, Friedhelm couldn't tell.

The boats only left at nighttime. The refugees needed the cover of darkness if they were to have any hope of making it out of the harbor into the open water without falling under Russian attack. August asked one of the boat captains about getting passage out of the city, and the captain advised the family to find shelter in a nearby apartment building overlooking the harbor. From there they would be able to watch the ships come and go, and they would be close by whenever a new boat arrived, which would increase their odds of successfully finding a boat with available space.

They followed the captain's directions to the entrance foyer of a three-story apartment building. The place was filled with soldiers under strict orders to defend the city to the death. Though they were vastly outnumbered by the surrounding Russians and had almost no remaining ammunition, they were not permitted to leave the city, and they were not allowed to surrender. Friedhelm remembered the bodies of deserters hanging in the city park, a dire warning to any soldier who might consider desertion.

So these troops—there were officers and nurses among them too—had taken over the apartment building while they waited for the impending invasion. Tobacco smoke and noise filled the foyer as soldiers walked up and down the stairs from one floor to the next. They smoked every cigarette, drank every last drop of liquor, gorged themselves on whatever food they could find, and danced to a phonograph they played over and over. Friedhelm was struck by the expressions on their faces, the frozen resignation in their eyes. These men knew, beyond a doubt, that they were soon to die. Yet they had no choice but to remain. So they bonded together, played loud music, ate from giant platters of food, and resolute in the face of death, enjoyed what worldly pleasures they could. They threw a party.

It was the last party they would ever attend.

At nightfall, August gathered the family and ushered everyone back to the harbor. The boats had just come in. If they were going to find passage out of the city, this would be their best chance.

As they piled into the area where people assembled to wait for the boats, guards inspected each person hoping to escape the city. A guard approached August. "I know you. You're from Kolberg."

"That's right," the old man answered. "I'm from Kolberg."

"Then why shouldn't you stay and fight?" the guard asked him. "Are you a coward?"

Friedhelm watched as his grandfather answered carefully. "I am no coward. I am seventy-one years old, and I have had a good life here in Kolberg. I am not afraid to lose it here. This war has already claimed the life of my wife—we laid her to rest just last week. But my daughter and her children need me now, and I am going with them so that they may escape. I want my family to live. That's what I am fighting for. My life in Kolberg is over. Now I will fight for the life my family has yet to live."

This seemed to move the guard. He nodded, and the entire family was allowed onto one of the boats.

It was a small boat, and it slipped quietly out of the dock and into the cold, black water of the Baltic Sea. When they were about a mile from shore, the boat lined up next to a large freighter. Black waves lapped gently at the sides of both boats. The night was so dark that Friedhelm could barely make out the freighter even once they were directly beside it. One by one, the passengers climbed up a ladder to the freighter's deck, and from there, they were shepherded below deck.

"Friedhelm!" his mother whispered in the dark. She and Brunhild were standing by the freighter's railing on the main deck, hidden in the darkness. Many people were being crammed into the hold of the ship, but Gertrud had no intention of going down there. Better to face the cold of the night, she reasoned, than to be trapped down there with whatever unforeseeable chaos they would encounter, not to mention the germs that would find them in such close quarters.

Her father had already climbed several steps down the stairs leading into the storage area below, but Gertrud grabbed hold of her son and daughter, knowing them by the shape of their hands. The three of them found a discreet spot on the main deck, out of everyone's way, where they huddled under blankets and waited for the ship to lift anchor.

It was an hour, maybe more, before the ship finally started moving westward into the Baltic Sea. The churn of its engines drowned out the noise of the distant artillery over Kolberg, but as Friedhelm looked back to the silhouetted skyline of the town, he saw something he would never forget: The Russian tanks and artillery surrounding the town had begun a coordinated attack. There were flashes of light from all sides of the town. The bombs cascaded down, and within minutes, the entire town of Kolberg, from one end to the other, was engulfed in a huge fireball. The city burned fiery orange against the coal-black sky.

Beside him, Gertrud felt a sob well up in her chest but choked it back down, determined to stay strong for the sake of her children. She was grateful her father was not on deck to see this. His life, his home, his legacy, even his wife's grave so freshly dug in the sand—everything he'd ever known was burning, destroyed by the ravenous flames. Kolberg as they knew it was gone forever.

Friedhelm felt his mother plant a kiss on his forehead. He looked up at her and saw her face tinted orange from the burning city across the sea. In her eyes he saw a strange mix of grief and gratitude. He understood exactly how she felt.

They had escaped, and just in time.

CHAPTER 23

HAMBURG: APRIL–MAY 1945

DURING THE FIRST DAYS of April, the bombs rained down on Hamburg without relenting. The air raid sirens went off day and night, and each time, the Job family would stop whatever they were doing and rush fearfully from the converted school to the bomb shelter, never knowing whether their temporary home would still be standing when they returned.

They spent as much time inside the shelter during those first days of April as they did out of it. They huddled closely together inside, praying or just listening, and they developed a sort of grim camaraderie with their neighbors, whose faces had become more and more familiar during those long, terrible nights and days.

The bombs themselves were only one part of the danger. Even after the Allied planes had turned around and flown home, the fires lit by their incendiary bombs raged on, spreading from one building to another until whole city blocks, whole neighborhoods, were destroyed.

We are blessed, Ludwig would remind himself and his children, *to have even the meager things we have. We are blessed even to be alive.*

Suddenly, on April 13, the air raid sirens stopped. The family slept peacefully through the night for the first time in two weeks. The next day, they all waited in anticipation of the screaming sirens, and the sirens never came.

Then another night passed the same way, and another day. For five days and nights, there were no bombers over Hamburg.

Ludwig didn't trust that the lull would continue. He knew the bombers might return at any time. But his children were less circumspect and more jubilant.

"Daddy, can we go outside?"

Elizabeth had been given a pair of roller skates by a woman at church, and she was eager to try them out. She knew of a street nearby that was smooth pavement, where there were absolutely no cars or even people because all the neighboring buildings had been destroyed and abandoned. "Can I go roller skating? Please?"

Eveline shrugged. "We can't keep them cooped up inside forever."

But before he let the children loose to play in their makeshift playground of rubble and ruins, Ludwig tuned into his radio to try to get some news—and that's how he finally learned why the bombing had stopped.

British tanks and infantry were beginning their assault on the city. They had already attacked the quarter of Harburg in the north and the town of Uelzen to the south and were advancing to the River Elbe. They had called off their air raids in order to begin a ground attack.

"We can and will keep them cooped up inside!" Ludwig answered Eveline. "At least for now."

The German forces that were left to defend the city were an assembled mix of SS, paratroopers, regular Wehrmacht soldiers, and Volkssturm militia recruited in recent months, along with the still-enthusiastic but almost wholly untrained Hitler Jugend. They didn't have the numbers or the training to prevent the British invasion, but they were under orders to make a last stand in Hamburg and never surrender, so they were digging into their fortifications and preparing for a long fight.

The city was about to become very unsafe indeed.

In between bombing raids, which usually came at night, Ludwig and others went to work. Life had to go on. But the decision had been made to keep the plant closed once the Allied forces were to start their attack on the city. Ludwig took a quick trip to shut down his lab. Then he returned to his family.

Together, they gathered around the radio to listen for any news about the invasion. Eduard had the idea to pull out the encyclopedia they had managed to ship from Warsaw, the *Meyers Grosses Konversationslexikon*. He opened it to a map of Hamburg, and with this and the information from the radio, the family was able to imagine how the front line was moving and how close the fighting was to their own location.

"This is good, right?" Eveline asked Ludwig quietly, while the children were distracted by the radio. "As soon as the Allies arrive, the war is over for us."

"Yes, that will most certainly be good. The British will free us from this war." He stopped himself. Should he say what he was thinking at this moment? That Allied victory would set them free not only from this war, but also from an iron sway that had held them captive far too long to genocidal actions and to an ideology that had forced them to give up personal freedom? Instead, he added what was uppermost in his mind this very moment: "It just remains to be seen what state we will all be in when they get here." He didn't know the best way to protect his family from the coming attack. "We will stay inside and stay as safe as we can."

The family stayed busy. They followed the radio reports closely, and when there were lulls in the news, they flipped through the *Konversationslexikon,* sharing articles with one another and quizzing each other on what they'd read. The battle outside progressed slowly, still far enough off that they rarely saw or heard any direct signs of it. Two weeks had gone by.

But then, during the night of the twenty-eighth of April, the rumble of a large explosion filled the air. It wasn't a sound like an air raid or artillery shell. It was something different—bigger—in the distance. Ludwig tuned his radio to get more information about what it might be.

He learned that the German forces had exploded the Autobahn, the main throughway in and out of Hamburg. In one more effort to slow the Allied advance, they were blowing up their own roads.

By morning, the battle had reached the city proper and was proceeding slowly, house by house. The ragtag German defense was fighting fiercely. They had no way, ultimately, of defeating the incoming forces, but they were making it very difficult for the British to proceed.

Then Ludwig's radio announced some unexpected news.

"The Führer, Adolf Hitler, has fallen at his command post in the Reich Chancery, fighting to the last breath against Bolshevism and for Germany."

"Hitler is dead." Ludwig repeated the words, for a moment unbelieving. Then he hugged his wife. "Hitler is dead!" He was surprised to discover his own feelings of relief, and for the first time in a long while, hope.

Hitler was where all of their troubles had begun. Hitler was why Warsaw had become unsafe for them and why the Russians had invaded and driven the Jobs from Poland. Hitler was why they were refugees. Hitler was why the Allies had bombed Hamburg so mercilessly. Now they might truly have a chance at a new start, because with Hitler gone, the German military would be free to negotiate a surrender. With Hitler gone, the poisonous words of hatred for the Jews would no longer spew forth over the radio, the flag with the swastika symbol would no longer represent the nation, and the propaganda lies would no longer treat them as fools.

Eveline threw herself into Ludwig's arms while the radio repeated the announcement again and again.

Outside in the streets the battle continued, but from what they could tell through the radio, the fighting seemed less intense than it had been. The soldiers on both sides sensed that the end was near.

Two days later, the highly decorated Luftwaffe Generalmajor Alwin Wolz surrendered the city to the British, and the battle of Hamburg was over.

British troops entered the city unopposed, and the Jobs, like so many of the people of Hamburg, came down to the streets to greet them. They didn't think of the soldiers as invaders. They thought of them as liberators—liberators from this abominable war.

While the victorious troops marched by in their khaki uniforms, carrying the British flag, they smiled at the people who had lined up along the street, and they stopped to say hello to the children. These were the first British men the children had ever seen. "Hello," the British men said in their funny English language, passing out sticks of chewing gum. "Hello," the children called back, trying to mimic the sound of the word.

Ludwig and Eveline stood in the street with their arms around one another. The arrival of the British in Hamburg meant the end of the war. They were truly safe now.

A few days after the Allies arrived, a British officer came to the school where they were living. His unit needed to set up offices, and there were few buildings left standing in Hamburg. He had been tasked with inspecting the school to see if it would be suitable for the unit's needs.

As he made his way through the building, he came upon little Elizabeth Job, playing by herself in a hallway near the school's staircase. He stopped in his tracks; the little girl reminded him so much of his own daughter.

Elizabeth had been told by her parents that the British were now their friends, and she smiled at the officer. He bowed down to her, and she could tell from his signs and movements that he was talking about his own little girl back in England. He even pointed with his index finger to his cheek. Because she thought it might make him happy, she kissed the British man there on the cheek. He smiled at her, wiped tears from his eyes, and then went on his way.

The Jobs were notified that the British needed to make use of the school building. Everyone living there would have to go. They suddenly needed to find housing again somewhere in this vast, ruined city.

The Philips Corporation had a number of employees who had lost their housing during the bombing raids, and the company took it upon itself to help find a place for these families to live. Philips owned some land that they used for storage, with a set of long, rectangular, hut-like barracks. One of those barracks had a long hallway from one end to the other with about five large rooms on either side, each divided from the other by a thin wall. The corporation vacated that structure and allowed the Jobs and several other employees and their families to live in it.

It wasn't especially well suited for use as an apartment. There were no kitchens, no sinks, and no private bathrooms, only a common restroom—and one couldn't shake the feeling that every conversation was being overheard by the next-door neighbors through the paper-thin walls. Ludwig and Eveline got into the habit of speaking Polish whenever they did not want their neighbors on either side to hear what was being said.

The Jobs were given one of the larger rooms in the barrack. As she'd done at their prior lodging, Eveline went to work to make the space homier for her family. She again divided up the room using military wardrobes so the four children and the parents could sleep on their narrow military beds in separate areas of the room. This left them the center of the room to use as a common area, which she designated as a dining room. They had a rough table to use, and though there weren't any cooking facilities, by now Eveline had acquired a two-burner electric stovetop that plugged into the wall, so she had herself a makeshift kitchen.

They had been surprised, months ago, to reunite with one of the packages they had shipped to themselves from Warsaw. While they were making their own way across Germany, their package had arrived at the Philips administrative office, and when Eveline unpacked it, she found many familiar remnants of home, including a full set of silverware and crystal. When she added these to their rough little kitchen in the barracks, the place didn't look so bad.

They were also delighted to discover they lived just a short walk from Hagenbecks Tierpark: the famous Hamburg Zoo.

The Hamburg Zoo was one of the first zoos in the world where animals were free to roam within large enclosures instead of inside cages, and it had been a real marvel throughout Europe before the war. It had stayed open throughout the war—closed to the public during the bombings, of course, while the animals were ushered inside for their protection. But the zoo had mostly escaped bombing damage, and when the air raids stopped and the Allies entered the city, the zoo was reopened and free to the public.

The children loved spending time at the zoo and went several times a week. The zoo also hosted puppet shows, which for children so starved for entertainment and education, were a real feast. People would sit in the audience holding paper lanterns lit with candles, each one on the end of a short stick. After the puppet show they would all parade out of the zoo, these golden lights bobbing in front of them, and then slowly scatter back into the city and into the night.

Back home in the barrack, as their children blew out their candles and went to bed and darkness settled, Eveline smiled at her husband and leaned her head on his shoulder. They were still refugees, still homeless. But they were alive. They clasped hands and listened to their children breathe, and they thanked God for bringing them so far. The Jobs lived in a world without government and without much certainty, but for now it was a safe and even wonderful time. They were together as a family, and they had survived the most destructive war that history had ever known.

CHAPTER 24

NORDHORN: SPRING 1945

FOR TWO DAYS after they boarded a ship in the Baltic Sea, the freighter carrying Gertrud and her two younger children out of Kolberg slowly made its way west.

Friedhelm watched from where his family huddled larboard near the bow of the ship. The sea was calm, and there were no other vessels in sight all the way to the horizon—yet the freighter often slowed to an almost complete halt in the open water.

"What's happening? Why aren't we moving?" he asked one of the crew members.

"Captain needs to take it slow, boy. The sea is full of mines and Russian submarines that have already sent a lot of ships like ours to the bottom of the ocean. There are thousands of other refugee boys just like yourself who never finished their voyage. So you let the captain go as slow as he wants to go, and maybe we'll all get to port in one piece."

The freighter was now west of the Oder River, back in territory that was still under German control. From the port side of the ship, Friedhelm could look out over the railing and get a clear view of the towns they passed along the Baltic Coast, the high bluffs, the white beaches, and the occasional lighthouse.

As he wondered what the names of these towns were, he felt a hand touching his shoulder from the back and heard his grandfather's voice: "We must be approaching the harbor town of Swinemünde."

Just then the freighter reached the tall lighthouse that marked the entrance into the Swine River, which would take them past the harbor and resort town of Swinemünde. That's where both August and Friedhelm stared at a city of still smoldering burned-out buildings, a devastating destruction that Allied bombing had caused just a few days earlier, on the twelfth of March. War showed its ugly face everywhere and seemed to accompany them on their escape. It was a face that would stay with Friedhelm and his grandfather for a long time to come.

August turned Friedhelm around so he would look west where he could see a vast, flat expanse of neatly fenced meadows, clusters of tall shrubs, and now and then a church steeple indicating the location of a village: a secluded landscape. His grandfather pointed out that a mere twenty kilometers from here, in Peenemünde, the V2 rockets had been first built and tested. "Those V2s were going to bring about total victory for Germany," he remarked quietly.

The sun climbed higher in the sky, and the freighter glided through a canal, known as the Kaiserfahrt, into the Stettiner Haff, a large lagoon along the Oder River. Flowering trees graced the lagoon's southern shoreline. Spring was coming to this part of Germany.

"It looks so peaceful," Friedhelm said to his grandfather. "From here, you can't even tell there is a war."

August nodded. "Your grandmother loved this part of the country for its serenity. I'm sorry she's not here with us to see it. But I'm grateful, too, that God took her when he did. She could never have made this journey with us, sick as she was. So she left us, and gave us time to say our good-byes too, before we had to leave Kolberg. Even the sad things in life often have blessings hidden inside them."

After two days, the ship finally docked in the inland harbor town of Ückermünde, and all the refugees disembarked. There they were immediately greeted by an organized group of townspeople in charge of refugee assistance. The refugees were paired with local families who took them in, fed them, and gave them a place to sleep for several days. The contrast between the peace and order of Ückermünde and the chaos of war they had just fled could not have been more stark.

It was while in Ückermünde that the Radandts learned how thoroughly Kolberg had been destroyed and how narrow their own escape had been. The damage was so bad, it was assumed by many that no one had made it out alive. All of Grandfather Rattunde's neighbors and friends who hadn't made it to the harbor in time were likely gone.

Gertrud wrote a quick note to her husband. She didn't know where the family would wind up, but she needed him to know that they had escaped Kolberg and that they were safe. "As soon as we know where we'll be, I will let you know." She addressed the letter to Pavia, Italy, where Ernst's unit was stationed, but she had no way to know if he was still there or if the letter would reach him.

Following several days of rest, the refugees were asked to report to the local railroad station. Their layover in the hospitable town was over, and now German authorities were working to find them a more permanent home. An official ushered them aboard a train, one person per seat, no more. This was no overcrowded refugee train. It was an orderly, calm, thoroughly planned relocation.

Once the train was full, it rolled out of the station. "Where are we going?" Friedhelm asked his mother, but no one seemed to know the answer. Despite all the order and planning, no one seemed to know the train's ultimate destination.

The train moved slowly westward. Sometimes, as it passed through a station, it would slow almost to a halt, and volunteers at the station would reach through the window to offer sandwiches and soup to the refugees inside. But the train would keep moving through the station without stopping.

The passengers onboard weren't allowed to disembark; the conductors responsible for ferrying the refugees couldn't afford the disorder of so many people coming and going. When the train did come to a complete stop, it was often in the open country, in between destinations—and it was almost always to avoid Allied bombing. The train rerouted away from both Berlin and Hamburg to avoid air strikes and instead took a path to the north through Mecklenburg and on toward Bremen, where it finally stopped briefly to take on coal for fuel.

Each time they passed through a town, Friedhelm made a mental note of its name. Most were places he'd never heard of. He recognized the name of the city of Bremen and remembered from his maps that this was deep in the heart of western Germany, farther than his family had ever traveled, so far from his home in Pomerania.

After three days like this, the train arrived in the town of Nordhorn, in the northwest corner of Germany, right on the Dutch border. It would become their new home.

The refugees were greeted by a number of locals and split into different groups. Friedhelm and his family and two dozen others rode with a set of farmers to a small restaurant on the outskirts of town. There, ladies stood ready to serve everyone a satisfying meal. They offered soup and delicious bread slices with liver sausage, cheese, and smoked ham. Strange to Friedhelm's ears, with each other these ladies spoke a language that he did not understand, although when they spoke to him or his mother, their German sounded normal. They were, so it seemed, most comfortable making use of their Low German dialect, but they were fully in command of the official High German. After serving everyone, the townspeople got to know the various refugee families and then paired them the best they could with different host families.

One of the townspeople, a gentle man named Farmer Menken, approached Friedhelm and asked if the boy had any interest in farm work. He explained that he ran a farm in the nearby village of Hesepe and could really use help, as his own sons had been enlisted in the war.

Friedhelm's eyes opened wide. He couldn't believe what he was hearing.

"I love living on a farm," he told this kind man. "Last summer I stayed on a farm for two weeks. That was fun, and I helped working in the fields."

"Where was that?" the farmer wondered, but he seemed pleased with the answer he'd received.

"The farm was in the village of Gramenz, not far from my hometown of Neustettin." They both agreed, and Friedhelm moved to the Menken farm. The other villagers then found a room for Gertrud and Brunhild, just eight minutes from Farmer Menken's, and Grandfather Rattunde was invited to stay in another house right next door to them. Within hours of their arrival in Nordhorn, they had all found temporary homes.

Friedhelm liked Farmer Menken, but he was nervous to be split up from his family. His grandfather took him aside. "This is a good town, Friedhelm. There is a Baptist Church here. We can stay here. We can make a home."

Friedhelm rode back that day with Farmer Menken and settled into his new life on the farm, where he enjoyed his own room and a comfortable bed. Each day Farmer Menken gave him new responsibilities—feeding the horses, caring for the chickens, raking the farmyard—until, very soon, Friedhelm felt like he knew his way around. Each evening he cleaned the huge stone floor in the kitchen and dining area. He did so by sprinkling some moist sand on the floor before sweeping it up. They liked his work and his company, which gave him a sense of usefulness and pride.

Farmer Menken also taught him some of the local traditions and cuisines. Friedhelm learned to bake a wonderful pumpernickel bread that cooked in the oven for two full days until it turned a deep, toasted brown. He learned to make pancakes the local way, with bits of bacon fried right into the batter.

There was so much good food. Even though Germany was still subject to war rationing, the farms outside Nordhorn produced and enjoyed a great bounty. Friedhelm and his family enjoyed bigger and better meals than they had in some time, including potatoes, meat dishes, butter, and milk, as well as cakes. To celebrate the spring and the upcoming Easter holiday, Farmer Menken even hosted an egg-eating competition, a contest to see who could eat the most hard-boiled eggs the fastest. Friedhelm hadn't seen such joyous eating since before the beginning of the war—if ever.

Now that she had an address, Gertrud penned another letter to her husband and posted it to him in Pavia. She wanted him to know they were safe in idyllic Nordhorn, so he would be able to find them when the war was over. If he ever got her letters, she had no way to know.

She also had no way to reach her other children. The last she had seen Ernst-August had been that terrible night they'd first fled Neustettin. She had asked him to desert the NSKK and come with the rest of the family, and he had refused. Since then, who knew what had become of her boy and his unit? Had he escaped the Russians and fled west, like they had? Or had he fallen into enemy hands?

Gisela, she knew, was safely situated with the Schütze family. She took comfort in knowing that the Schützes were very responsible and would do everything within their power to protect Gisela and provide for her safety. But there were too many unknowns. No family could promise protection against the madness of war. What had happened to the Schützes when the Russians invaded Pomerania? Had they managed to escape? And if so, where? How would she ever find Gisela across this vast, war-torn country?

She desperately wanted to find her children and didn't know how. For now, it was all she could do to try to get in touch with her husband. Maybe when the war was over they would be able to sort everything else out.

On April 1, the family walked into town to celebrate Easter at Nordhorn's Baptist church, and they were invited to join one of the local families for an Easter dinner. It was that church and its wonderful people that made Nordhorn a true home for the Radandts, and they quickly became active, valued members of the Baptist community there. When a room became available in the parsonage, the pastor and his wife invited Gertrud and Brunhild to move in.

In the meantime, the war was still going on. The Allied troops were getting closer to the Dutch border. Every night, bombers flew over Nordhorn, but they never dropped any payload. They were en route to some other target. Friedhelm sat on the east side of the Menken farmhouse, and looking over the long, flat fields, watched the planes overhead and followed them as they disappeared into the horizon. Then, three or four hours later, he saw them flying back in the other direction, their mission complete.

Nobody in the Menken farmhouse ever spoke to Friedhelm about the Führer or the Nazis. But he could tell by their whispers that they were ready to welcome the Allied forces as liberators, and when they asked about his siblings—especially his brother in the NSKK—and his father, they did so with great concern for their safety.

One night the raid was much closer to home, striking at a small airstrip just seven miles from the Menken farm. The airstrip was home to one small, single-engine plane that went up in the air each morning—presumably on some government or military business, because there was no other way the plane could have secured fuel for its flying. Likely the plane was running reconnaissance missions to monitor weather and troop movements in the area.

The bombers targeted the little airstrip, and Friedhelm and Farmer Menken watched the bombs fall for a half-hour like they were far-off fireworks.

Then, the next morning, the two of them stared out the window in wonder as that little single-engine plane took off from the tiny airstrip as if the bombing raid had never happened. All the fireworks had been for nothing; the airstrip and the little plane were both fully operational.

The Allies took the city of Nordhorn a few days before the middle of April, and the people of Hesepe knew it would be only a short time before the troops secured the city and then expanded into the countryside. Several of Farmer Menken's neighbors began gathering at his farm, assembling in the barn adjoining the farmhouse so they would all be in one central place whenever the Allies arrived. They hung a white flag on the barn door as a clear indication to the incoming Allies that they had no intention of fighting back, and then they stretched a long extension cord through the house to the barn, where they all huddled around the Volksempfänger, waiting for news.

In the morning of the eleventh of April, a troop of German soldiers came through the fields around the farm. A German sergeant tore down their white flag and stormed into the barn. "You should be ashamed!" he yelled at them, throwing the white flag at their feet. "You should stand up for Germany!"

The soldiers hollowed out foxholes in a small forest beside the Menken farm, and dug in for what Friedhelm assumed must be an imminent invasion. But no invasion came, and as suddenly as they'd appeared, the soldiers left the foxholes and marched on. Friedhelm never saw them again.

Once they were gone, Farmer Menken hung the white flag back on the barn and resumed waiting by the radio. He was a peaceable man, and he didn't want any trouble. They expected to hear news of incoming Canadian and British tanks, but instead, on the thirteenth of April, 1945, they heard an unexpected announcement from Joseph Goebbels, the Reich Minister of Propaganda: "Roosevelt, the greatest war criminal of all time, is dead."

The American president had fallen.

Before Friedhelm could consider what this meant or what bearing it had on his current situation, he heard a rumble from outside the window, getting louder. A line of jeeps was approaching the farm. The Allied troops had arrived.

Farmer Menken stepped into his doorway with his hands in the air. "We're here," he said. "We surrender."

Friedhelm watched as a few soldiers approached and spoke with Farmer Menken. For Friedhelm and his family, the war was over at last. But there were still many unknowns. Was his father a prisoner of war? Had his brother and sister been captured by the Russians? How would any of them ever find the family in Nordhorn? Until they were reunited, or at least had answers, how could they begin building their lives in this new home?

Though the war was over, Friedhelm realized, his family was still a long way from living in peace.

CHAPTER 25

((•))

ALT-KARBE: SPRING 1945

THEY HAD STAYED because of a zipper machine.

When the Jobs fled the town of Bärwalde at the end of January 1945 to avoid the imminent Russian invasion, they never imagined they were boarding the last train out of town. Eveline's family—her mother Eugenia Witt, her sister Frieda, and Frieda's family, the Rosners—intended to board the next train out of town.

But first they needed to hide the machine.

Eugenia, along with Frieda's family—her husband Herbert Rosner and their three daughters, and Herbert's brother Gustav Rosner and his family—had left Poland in the summer of 1944. Gustav had decided that it would be best if they closed down their zipper company in Lodz, and he shipped their machinery to Germany. Their plan was to restart production in the city of Wuppertal, but once they moved there they discovered that the intensity of the Allied bombing raids made that impossible.

When they moved again in early January 1945, they left their machinery behind in Wuppertal, except for one special machine that would allow them to begin limited production and so rebuild their livelihood. It represented a significant investment and meant they would have a good start on a new future.

So, on the morning of January 30, when the radio warned them of an imminent Russian invasion, the Rosners took some time to hide and secure their machine before heading to the train station.

But the Red Army had advanced much more quickly than anyone expected. By the time the Rosners arrived at the station, it was overrun with people trying to get out of town, and there were no more trains going in or out.

While everyone around them panicked, the Rosners simply took their bags back home and unpacked them. They tidied up and changed into their nicest clothes. While the town devolved into chaos, the Rosners brewed a pot of tea and waited quietly for the Russian army to arrive.

They had heard the horror stories, of course, about the treatment that German citizens received when they fell into the hands of Soviet soldiers. But both the Rosners and Eugenia Witt had one advantage that many of their neighbors in Bärwalde did not have.

They had lived eight years of their lives in Russia, exiled in Siberia. They had attended Russian schools. They spoke the Russian language beautifully. They knew how to interact with Russian officials.

So when the Red Army's tanks rolled into town and the infantry marched through the streets, banging on door after door, the Rosners simply opened their home and, in perfect Russian, invited the officers inside for some tea.

Imagine the surprise of the Russian officers after so many weeks of brutal hostility. They were so grateful to receive such polite hospitality, they immediately warmed to the Rosners and offered them protection against the onslaught of the foot soldiers.

It was the beginning of an accidental, ingenious plan: from the moment the Russians arrived in Bärwalde, the Rosners simply ceased to be German. Instead, they reidentified themselves as Poles who had fond memories of their time in Russia. This wasn't even a lie, exactly. Though they had always thought of themselves as German and now carried German citizenship papers, they had spent their entire lives as citizens of Poland. So they were Polish too.

It was a ruse that would save them some trouble in the short term, but too many people in Bärwalde knew the Rosners as Volksdeutsche, ethnic Germans, for their lie to go unnoticed for long. They realized that if they could move out of town, somewhere farther east, then they could settle in a place where no one knew their history. In a new town they could start over—as non-Germans.

The entire extended family—the two families of Rosners along with Eugenia Witt—packed their bags, negotiated for some horses, and rode in covered wagons on roads that pointed back toward Poland—until they came upon a town called Alt-Karbe in southern Pomerania. Alt-Karbe, like the rest of the region, had already been captured by the Russians, but this town was essentially empty when the Rosners arrived. Its former population of Germans had evacuated and fled west before the Russian invasion.

In other words, it was a town that had been emptied of its history. It was a perfect place for the Rosners to start over and reinvent themselves as non-German Poles.

As soon as they arrived in town, they were required to report to the local Russian commandant, who was so impressed with the Rosners' fluency in his language and with their managerial skills and work experience that he appointed the newly arrived Gustav Rosner the new mayor of the town. Gustav would act as the commandant's liaison with the local Polish people, who were expected to arrive in short order to take up residence in Alt-Karbe. The commandant didn't even care that the Rosners were actually Volksdeutsche; he needed people he could trust to help him manage the town, and he decided the Rosners were perfect for the job.

The commandant also appointed Herbert to an important job in town: it was his task to inventory all the town's valuables—its industrial equipment, quality furniture, silver, and china—and supervise the gradual shipment of those goods to Russia.

By spring, it was clear that the war was winding down, and it became known that the occupying Russian forces planned to redraw the borders of Poland and turn this formerly German region over to the Polish people. Many Polish citizens began to arrive in Alt-Karbe, eager to settle the town and rebuild the Polish nation—and the Rosners, the administrators of the town, became more and more entrenched in their false identities as non-German Poles.

They instructed their children to speak only Polish, ever. They told them to forget they even knew German and never speak it, and certainly never to mention to anyone that they were German.

They couldn't even imagine what would happen to them if the Polish townspeople discovered who they really were.

By summer, the town had been completely resettled and had taken on the feel of a traditional Polish town. Instead of its old German name of Alt-Karbe, it had been given the new Polish name of Stare Kurowo.

The town's streets were also given Polish names. Its stores were stocked with goods by their new Polish owners. The town's old Lutheran church was converted into a Catholic church. Its school was reopened, and classes were conducted exclusively in Polish. The Rosner children, keeping up their masquerade, attended the schools as if they were good little Polish students.

But elaborate lies are hard enough for adults to maintain, let alone for young children.

Every day, Herbert and Frieda's three daughters Welli, Dieta, and Inka, would go off to school to practice their reading, writing, and arithmetic, and every day, before they left, their mother Frieda would remind them never to breathe a word in German while they were there. The three daughters knew how important this was, and they were careful not to slip up.

But one morning, the schoolteacher wrote a multiplication problem on the board, and young Inka was so excited to know the answer before her classmates that she called out the answer—in German.

Inka was young, but not so young that she failed to notice the awkward silence that followed, or the teacher's strange and suspicious looks for the rest of the day.

When she returned home from school that day, she told her parents what had happened, and they decided they could not afford to take any chances. Gustav and his family were already out of town, having been invited by a Russian officer to accompany him to Dresden. So as soon as dusk fell, Herbert rode his bike to the nearby town of Landsberg, to the house of the local Russian commandant, to explain the situation and ask for help.

Frieda waited inside the house with her daughters with the doors locked and the curtains drawn, but before her husband returned, a troop of Polish soldiers came to the house with their guns drawn and took the whole family into custody. In the soldiers' minds, these were the same people who had been stealing the town's valuables and exporting them to the Russians—and on top of that, now they were German.

Frieda and the children, along with Eugenia Witt, were locked in a windowless storage area while the local Polish authorities deliberated over their fate.

"What's going to happen to us?" fourteen-year-old Welli asked her mother. "What are we going to do?"

Frieda wanted to comfort her daughter, but she didn't know what to tell her. The Polish people were understandably upset. They had seen too much bloodshed and suffered too much abuse at the hands of the Germans over the past years. Frieda knew no way to quell their temper.

When words didn't come, she closed her eyes and reached out to hold her daughters' hands, and she began singing a church hymn they all knew. The girls joined her, and that is how they spent the night—singing hymns and holding one another and praying for deliverance and mercy. Welli would never forget her grandmother's fervent prayers, in part because they were spoken in Polish, the only language Eugenia Witt used in any of her prayers.

The next morning, a small Russian military convoy entered the town and took the Rosners out of custody. They drove the family to Landsberg, where Herbert was waiting for them with the Russian commandant. Then, after they had turned over to the Russians a hefty payment of a fur coat, several watches, and a lot of cash, a driver took the family to the nearby town of Gartz on the Oder River, in the Russian-occupied zone, with instructions to get out of the area for good. It was for their own safety.

In Gartz, the Rosners arrived early at the train station. This time they weren't taking any chances. They booked the first train to Berlin, and there they started their postwar life. After a failed experiment at being Polish, they were Germans once again.

CHAPTER 26

PAVIA: MAY 1945

"COME ON, ERNST. We have to go!"

Ernst Radandt's friend and coworker, Sebastian, called out from the passenger seat of the army car that the two of them had loaded up with files and sundry equipment from their office. Their unit had been given an evacuation order, and the caravan of cars and trucks was lining up, ready to pull out of town as soon as the sun set.

"Just one more sweep of the office, to make sure we haven't missed anything," Ernst answered.

"Do you always need to be so thorough? Even now?"

Ernst had been stationed in the Italian town of Pavia since the early summer of 1944, which meant he'd been working alongside Sebastian for nearly a year now. Sebastian had taken maybe a little too well to the lazy Italian sunshine. His friend had many qualities Ernst enjoyed, but thoroughness wasn't among them.

Ostensibly, their entire unit was in place in Pavia to support the German troops in their efforts to slow down the advance of the Allied armies coming up from the south and thus to prevent an Allied invasion of Austria and Germany through Italy. In reality, there never had been any real danger of that happening. The Allies were closing in on

Germany from both the east and the west, steadily and relentlessly. So Ernst's experience of the war had been relatively calm, except for the periodic, troubling news he received from his family back in Pomerania. He himself had never heard a shot fired, never seen an enemy soldier, and never had occasion to aim, let alone shoot, his own handgun. Meanwhile, his wife and children were seeing more threat of violence from the invading army than he had seen as a soldier, and he was powerless to protect them.

"I'll tell you what," Ernst told his friend. "If I'm gone for more than a few minutes, you can start the car yourself and drive away without me."

Sebastian rolled his eyes. The car's ignition was notoriously temperamental, and Ernst was the only one in the whole unit who could reliably get the engine to turn over. "I don't know how you trick this car into starting," Sebastian said.

"It's not a trick," Ernst laughed. "You simply have to show it a little love and respect."

"Just hurry!" Sebastian said, looking nervously at the line of trucks getting ready to roll out of town.

Ernst ducked one last time into his office. He had spent his entire year in Pavia working inside this little room. He woke to a bugle call each morning, put on his crisp, clean uniform, and reported to this office, where he and Sebastian mostly filed paperwork for the duration of the day. Except for being in sunny Italy, far from his family and worried about them, his life wasn't terribly different here than it had been in Pomerania. He showed up each day, read and organized a lot of bureaucratic letters and forms, and then went home.

He took a final look through all the desk drawers. He and Sebastian had cleaned out the office earlier that day, and everything was, as he'd guessed, scrupulously emptied already. But on his way back out of the building, he saw a small sack sitting hidden just behind the front door. The postman must have delivered one final batch of mail to the office that afternoon, not realizing they'd evacuated the place already.

Ernst grabbed the sack of mail and ran back outside. He climbed into the driver's seat and reached down toward the ignition. "Come on," he coaxed the car—and started the engine on the first try.

"I don't know how you trick this car into starting," Sebastian repeated, and Ernst smiled at him and drove up the narrow Italian street to take their place with their unit's caravan.

They were being called back to Germany. It was obvious to everyone now that the war was winding down, but no one in the unit knew if their orders were to return for one final defense of the Fatherland against the Allied invasion, or more simply to return as part of a surrender. All Ernst knew for sure was that he was to follow the caravan very closely on their drive up through the Alps, hugging the bumper of the truck in front of him as they wound through the serpentine mountain roads without headlights, on alert against any partisans. If they fell under attack on their drive back, they were practically defenseless, and they would almost certainly become prisoners of war—or worse.

Ernst kept a close eye on the road while Sebastian began combing through the mail sack he'd recovered. "Look," Sebastian said, holding up a letter from the sack. "One of these is addressed to you."

Ernst could tell from the handwriting on the envelope that it was a letter from Gertrud. "What does it say? Read it!"

Sebastian wasn't much of a reader, and he struggled a bit with Gertrud's handwriting in the dim glow of his flashlight, but the gist of the letter was clear: Gertrud, Friedhelm, and Brunhild had escaped Neustettin before the Russians arrived and made it out of Kolberg just before the deadly siege came to its end. They were secure in the town of Nordhorn, in northwestern Germany—a long way from home, but safe.

Ernst said a silent prayer of thanks while he drove the car through the Alps. Once the Russians had overrun Pomerania, he had lost track of his family. He'd had no idea how to find them again. For several weeks he had not received any mail from his family. Now he had an actual address for his wife and two of his children. They were safe.

If only he knew about the other two.

"You're not going to believe this," Sebastian told him.

His friend held up a second letter from the mail sack, from Ernst's daughter Gisela. She told her father of her harrowing escape in February from Rittergut Dolgen with the Schütze family and their dash across the frozen lake. Of all the people working and living at the estate, she said, only she and the Schützes, along with their white German shepherd dog, had managed to escape the Russians.

She described her long, cold journey on the refugee trek and her unlikely run-in with her brother Ernst-August, and how, several weeks later, the refugees had settled in the province of Schleswig-Holstein, north of Hamburg. She was staying now in a village called Hohenweststedt. Mr. Schütze in particular felt very bad about what had happened to Gisela, and he felt he'd failed the Radandts in his promise to keep their daughter safe. He was working very hard to find a suitable farming estate that would be willing to take her in and provide for her in the ways that the Schützes no longer could.

"Mr. Schütze hopes that you and Mother will forgive him these mishaps," Gisela wrote.

In fact, Ernst felt immeasurably grateful that the Schütze family had helped his daughter escape and brought her to safety. He was brokenhearted at the terrors his family had experienced in his absence, but he also found himself in tears of amazement: if he hadn't returned to his office that one final time, he would never have found the mailbag. But because he had, he now knew the whereabouts of his wife and had a rough idea where to find his daughter; he also had at least the assurance that his son Ernst-August had escaped Neustettin.

He now could name a town where he was headed next, once the war was over and he was free. *If God put this knowledge of Gertrud's address in my lap, will he not also grant us to become reunited once again?* As Ernst's lips formed this prayer, he knew that he would do everything in his power to make it to Nordhorn and then locate his children and reunite his family.

The caravan stopped in the town of Freilassing, not far from Salzburg. They had covered many miles of serpentine mountain roads and made it through the Alps back into Germany without falling into enemy hands. It was the eighth of May 1945, and Ernst's commanding officer had just received word over the radio that Germany had surrendered, unconditionally, to the Allies.

The war was over.

The commander, no longer in command, was at a bit of a loss for how to respond to the news, or what orders to give to these soldiers who were no longer soldiers. Finally he announced to all of them, "You are free men. Go home, if you have one, and God protect you."

The war was over, but they were hardly out of danger. Not all soldiers would necessarily have heard about the surrender. There was still some threat of violence. And despite the surrender, they were still a company of soldiers: if they fell into Allied hands, they would almost certainly be considered prisoners of war.

The commanding officer wanted them all to make it home safely, and to help them on their way, he allowed the soldiers to keep the cars and trucks they were driving—until they ran out of gas, were captured by the Allies, or arrived at their destinations.

"Well," Sebastian said to Ernst. "Where to now?"

"I need to go to Nordhorn," Ernst answered, and he pointed the car northwest.

They drove for an hour before coming upon a company of French troops. They had little choice but to stop. Ernst and Sebastian stepped out of their car and held their hands in the air. "I'm sorry, my friend," Sebastian said. "No Nordhorn for you. We're prisoners of war now for sure."

The French soldiers approached them and inspected their papers while Ernst and Sebastian stood silently waiting. Then, the French lieutenant surprised them and told them they were free to go. "War is over," was all he said.

But the Frenchmen insisted on confiscating the car. Ernst and Sebastian grabbed their belongings from the back seat and started walking up the road. Before they got too far, Ernst whispered to Sebastian and pulled him off the road to hide in the bushes. "Let's just wait a little longer." He pointed back to the French soldiers, who struggled in vain to get the car's engine to turn over. Eventually, the French gave up on the car, boarded their trucks, and drove away.

Ernst and Sebastian trotted back to the car, and Ernst turned the engine over on the first try. He winked at Sebastian. "Love and respect."

They drove north for several more hours before they ran out of gas. From there, they started walking. They carefully avoided main roads and talked with the German farmers they met to learn whatever they could about troop movements. The farmers were happy to help them on their way and offered them meals and a place to sleep while the two soldiers worked their way toward home.

Sebastian's family was from Frankfurt, and as soon as the two of them made it that far north, avoiding the city and its immediate environs, they parted company. They had walked together for over 250 miles over the last three weeks. "Thank you for the safe passage," Sebastian told Ernst with a hug.

But just north of Frankfurt, only hours after separating from his friend, Ernst walked right into a squad of American military police. He put his hands in the air and surrendered. They loaded him into the back of their jeep and drove him to a prisoner-of-war camp.

Upon his arrival at the camp, the Americans sent him to be interviewed by a German-speaking officer.

"Your German is excellent," Ernst told the man.

"My family is from Germany," the officer told him. "But we left because we're Jewish."

Ernst knew his surprise was visible on his face—and perhaps his fear. He knew that atrocities had been committed against the Jewish people, both before and during the war. He had also heard rumors that the atrocities had been much worse than he or others were able to imagine. And now his own fate was in the hands of a Jewish-American whose family had fled their home country because of those inhuman deeds.

The man asked him questions about his role in the war—where he had been stationed and how he had spent his time. Ernst answered each of the man's questions sincerely and honestly.

"And where were you headed when the soldiers apprehended you?"

"My family is in Nordhorn," Ernst answered simply.

The officer looked at Ernst intently. "You're forbidden to take up arms. Do you understand?"

"What?" Ernst was confused by the question. Were they letting him go? "Of course I won't. I just want to get back to my family."

The American nodded. "Good. Then let's get you back to your family."

Ernst could not believe it. Once again, he prayed his wordless thanks to God.

Within an hour, he was to board an American military truck bound for Münster, only forty-five miles from Nordhorn. It was just enough time for a brief medical exam and for lunch. Yes, the Americans had even arranged for some food before the drive north on the Autobahn. By the end of the day, Ernst was a free man in the city of Münster.

By June 2, 1945, three weeks after Germany's unconditional surrender, Gertrud still hadn't heard a word from her husband. She didn't know where he was, didn't know if he had fallen into enemy hands. She also didn't know if he had received any of her letters or if he knew how to find them. But that morning, the pastor's wife came to her at the breakfast table where they were living at the parsonage and asked Gertrud out of the blue, "Does your husband have big ears?"

Gertrud was perplexed. "Yes. As a matter of fact, he does."

"Then he is coming home to you today. I saw him in my dream."

Several hours later, a young girl stopped at the Menken farm and found Friedhelm where he was doing his chores. "You need to go to the parsonage. Your father has come home."

Friedhelm was stunned. Who was this girl? Was it true, what she was telling him about his father?

Farmer Menken lent him a bicycle, and Friedhelm pedaled as fast as he could into town. He banged on the door of the parsonage until his mother answered. "Where is Father?"

Again, Gertrud was perplexed. "I don't know. Why are you asking me that?"

No one knew anything about a girl. Puzzled, Friedhelm settled in for a visit with his mother. And then they looked out the window.

Ernst had gone straight to the address he'd found on Gertrud's letter—but she had written the letter before she moved to the parsonage. Gertrud and Brunhild were no longer at that address, but Gertrud's father, August Rattunde, was still living right next door. He greeted his son-in-law with a huge hug and led him to the parsonage.

So it was that Ernst Radandt, in his worn army uniform, exhausted, elated, feeling almost overwhelmed with gratitude, walked up the Lange Strasse to the parsonage of the Baptist church and reunited with his wife and children. They saw him through their window, coming up the street, and Friedhelm ran out to greet him and walked with him the last hundred yards or so, until Ernst walked through the door of the parsonage and fell into the arms of his wife.

The next day was Sunday, and the family arrived early at the Baptist church, together for the first time in years. In the coming months, Ernst would settle his family into the town of Nordhorn and begin the work of tracking down his two missing children.

But today, Sunday, his first day in Nordhorn, he went to church, and he gave thanks to God.

PART 3

CHAPTER 27

SCHLAGSDORF: 1945

ERNST RADANDT DID his best to settle into his family's new home, a room they shared inside an apartment that belonged to a baker and his wife in Nordhorn. Though it was a crowded and difficult way to live, a far cry from their lovely little house in Pomerania, still Ernst was grateful for it. He was grateful for all the good that had come out of so many bad experiences; grateful that his wife and children had escaped Neustettin; grateful that Gertrud had managed to flee to Kolberg and then escape that city before its destruction; grateful that they had found refuge among the Baptist community of Nordhorn; grateful that he had found his way back to them.

He was grateful, but he was not at peace.

Two of his children were still missing, and Ernst could find no peace until he had done his best to discover what had happened to them. He needed to know that they were safe, and if possible, he needed to bring them home.

Before that, if he were going to take care of his family in this new postwar world, he needed a job. Soon after his arrival in Nordhorn, he approached one of the farmers he'd met at the church. "I used to work on farms in Pomerania. Maybe you could use an extra hand?"

The farmer agreed to take him on. But Ernst was undernourished from the war. He hadn't done farm work in many years, and even when he had, he'd mostly acted as an administrator, not a laborer. After a few days working in the fields, he was in so much pain that he could barely walk. He badly wanted to work, but his body wouldn't allow it.

Another man from the church saw both Ernst's eagerness and his suffering, and he helped find him a job at a textile mill in town. The work was tedious and a bit mindless, but at least it was not so backbreaking.

What Ernst really wanted, though, was to make contact with Gisela wherever she was in Hohenweststedt and to find Ernst-August.

He wrote a letter to the mayor of the village of Hohenweststedt in Schleswig-Holstein, asking for information on Gisela's exact whereabouts. But in the months immediately following Germany's surrender, only very sporadic mail service served the country. Trains, for the most part, weren't running, and gasoline was still rationed. It was a long, frustrating time before Ernst was able even to *send* the letter he'd written.

Then he waited impatiently for a response.

Finally, he received an answer from the mayor of Hohenweststedt that brought him great relief: Gisela was still in the area, and the mayor included the name of the estate in Schleswig-Holstein where she was staying.

He wrote her immediately, to tell her that her family had survived and was living in Nordhorn. "I will come for you as soon as trains are running," he promised, "and I will bring you home."

He also told her that he had no knowledge of what had happened to her brother Ernst-August. He had already searched Red Cross records and bulletin announcements with news about refugees, and he'd found nothing useful. He was hoping that Gisela could put him in touch with Mr. Schütze. All the members of Ernst-August's unit had been from Neustettin, and surely the Schützes or one of their many contacts from that region would have some knowledge of what had happened to the boys in the unit. Even if they didn't know anything themselves, they might know someone who did.

Waiting on the slow mail service was almost unbearable, but before too long, Ernst received a reply from Gisela. She was happy to report that she was very well taken care of and was once again a nanny to some young children in a very supportive family.

She also knew how to reach the Schützes. Ernst wrote them a letter immediately. Then he sat down and prayed—fervently—asking God to grant his and Gertrud's burning desire to locate their older son.

Ernst thought a great deal about the events of the last twelve years. To be sure, for now Germany was without a government and under the control of the Allied forces, and his family were refugees. He thought about God and faith, and he came to see life in a new light.

It was on a late, warm August afternoon that summer of 1945 when Ernst put that new understanding into words for Friedhelm. The two had been out working the garden plot—right along the Vechte River—that one of the farmers in the Baptist church of Nordhorn let them use to grow food for the family. Before starting their walk home, they took a swim in the Vechte. After that swim Ernst spoke words that Friedhelm would never forget: "Here is something I want you to remember. God has always shed his grace on our family, just as he has been merciful with our country. But his mercy was at its greatest when he permitted Germany to be defeated. That's the reason we now can live life in freedom."

It took until autumn before Ernst received a reply from Mr. Schütze—a long letter. Most importantly, he had learned from his contacts in Neustettin that a number of men in the NSKK unit had indeed made it to the town of Ratzeburg, including its commander, Mr. Schreiber.

Ratzeburg, Ernst knew, was near the city of Lübeck, and right up against the newly erected Iron Curtain.

Progress was going too slowly. He had enough information now to know where to begin a search for his son, and he decided he needed to act. He would go to Ratzeburg and meet with Mr. Schreiber to find out what he knew about Ernst-August, then make his way to the estate in Schleswig-Holstein where Gisela was waiting.

But there were still no passenger trains running to Lübeck, just occasional freight trains. A textile truck from the factory where he worked drove Ernst part of the way, and from there he hopped on a freight train and rode it into Ratzeburg.

The same afternoon that Ernst arrived in town, he sat down with Mr. Schreiber.

"Your son is alive and well, and in fact, I know exactly where he is," Ernst-August's former commander told Ernst. "But I'm afraid you're not going to like it."

Ernst was unsure what to make of that ominous statement. He wanted to ask . . . but Mr. Schreiber—he had never before seen him without his NSKK Nazi uniform—excused himself for a moment. When he returned, he held a map of the area in his hand and placed it on the dining table, inviting Ernst to sit with him at the table.

Ernst-August's former commander began to tell the story of the last day he had seen Ernst-August, in early May at the very end of the war. "Our unit was approaching the city of Lübeck. We set up camp just west of the Trave Canal. But another part of our unit was still farther east, on the other side of the canal. I told your son to ride across the bridge that spanned the canal and deliver an order to that section of our unit, for them to meet up with us on this side of the canal, and reassemble in the town of Ratzeburg.

"That is the last I saw your son. You see, at that time the Russians were closing in on Lübeck, and that bridge was the only easy way for them to get into the city. As soon as Ernst-August crossed, the SS exploded it, cutting off his only way back. He was over there when the Allies attacked."

Ernst was shaken by the man's story. "But he survived?"

"Oh, yes," Schreiber reassured him. "He got caught in what must have been a terrible battle. But he survived. He lives now with a farmer in the village of Schlagsdorf."

On the map in front of him, Schreiber showed Ernst the location of the village and of the town of Ratzeburg. "You see, it's only an hour's walk from where we are in Ratzeburg. But do you see your problem?"

The man used his index finger to draw an imaginary line down the map. "Lübeck, the Trave—this is the easternmost territory in the British sector. Schlagsdorf, where your son is—that is Soviet territory. No going in or out."

"I must get to my son," Ernst told him.

"No," Schreiber shook his head. "Mr. Radandt, you have other family. What happens to them if you go there"—he pointed to Schlagsdorf—"and you cannot make it back here? A trip into the Russian zone is something you cannot and should not undertake."

Ernst nodded. Though his heart was breaking, he understood that the man was right.

"But," Schreiber continued, "I do know some people, young people without as much to lose as yourself, who make this crossing each week. They will be leaving after the sun has set and will be in Schlagsdorf late tonight."

It was an unexpected hope.

By that evening, Mr. Schreiber had introduced Ernst to two young men willing to act as messengers. The men knew the farm where Ernst-August was staying, and they thought they might even have seen him once or twice, driving a horse-drawn carriage full of Russian officers through Schlagsdorf.

"If that boy is your son, then we will get a message to him," they promised. "What do you want us to tell him?"

"Tell him to meet his father on the west side of the border at seven o'clock tomorrow morning."

((ǂ))

Ernst-August was indeed living in Schlagsdorf. The day he'd ridden his motorcycle east across the Trave Canal and out of Lübeck, the day the SS destroyed the bridge and made it impossible for him to return, he had driven on to complete his mission. He found the straggling section of NSKK gathered with several thousand other German soldiers in a field, all of them awaiting what they imagined would be the imminent arrival of Allied troops and the end of the war, unsure whether it would be Russian or British troops.

But as Ernst-August arrived, the unit immediately came under an unexpected attack from a squadron of low-flying British fighter planes. Their engines roared overhead, and they opened fire.

Ernst-August found himself in the middle of a battle.

He ran with the other soldiers into a nearby patch of woods, but it didn't offer much cover. The planes kept circling back, and each time they did, they sprayed the area with machine-gun fire. Ernst-August crouched low, huddled in a small ditch near a tree, watching each time the planes passed, watching the trail of bullets striking the dirt, listening to the screams of his fellow soldiers who were hit by the strafing.

The attack lasted for four unbearable hours. Each time the planes flew by, Ernst-August prayed their bullets would somehow miss him, and once the planes had passed, he thanked God that he had escaped unhurt. The odds of surviving the attack seemed almost impossible—there just wasn't enough cover—but somehow the bullets missed him every time. Finally the planes went past and didn't circle back; they were either out of fuel or out of ammunition.

He took off his shirt to look for any signs of injury. He seemed to be unharmed, but he couldn't stop shaking. He remembered the conversation he'd had with his mother outside Neustettin. He was just a boy, she'd told him. He didn't need to be a soldier. He didn't need to die in an adults' war.

For the first time, he admitted to himself that she was right.

He still had those civilian clothes in his backpack, and his uniform was half-off already. When none of the other soldiers were looking, he reached into his pack and changed into his street clothes.

And not a moment too soon. While he was still buttoning up his shirt, he heard the growl of Allied tanks approaching. They had to be British tanks, and sure enough, they were. The German soldiers put down their weapons and threw their arms into the air. Here, at the end, they felt relief. They knew it was far better to fall into British hands than to be captured by the Russians.

Ernst-August put his hands up into the air. "I surrender!" he shouted to the British infantrymen who walked nearby.

The soldiers just chuckled and walked right past him. All they saw was a boy dressed in civilian clothes. He was no threat to them. "Go on, lad," an officer told him. "Go home."

Go home. Ernst-August had taken several years of English at the Fürstin Hedwig Oberschule in Neustettin and knew exactly what the soldier was telling him. But he also knew he didn't have a home to go to. His hometown of Neustettin was overrun with Russians. He knew his family had made it out, but he had no idea what had happened to them in the months since their escape. And he had no way to reach them.

He was free, but he had nowhere to go.

Unsure what to do or where to head, he walked in the direction of Ratzeburg, where the rest of his NSKK unit was positioned, but he quickly realized that even if he could find them, reuniting with them was not an option so long as the war was on. Now that he'd gotten rid of his uniform, they would consider him a deserter.

He was coming up on a village called Schlagsdorf, and he figured it was as good a place as any for him to stop and consider his next steps. When he arrived in the village, he learned he had no choice but to stay. It was the eighth of May. The British soldiers told him he could go no further. Germany had surrendered, and the Allies had ordered a halt to all movement for the next two days while they secured the area and sorted out the logistics of the new situation.

Ernst-August was a fourteen-year-old boy stuck in a village where he had no family, no friends, no food, and no shelter. But he did have some skills and an uncanny knack for charming people. He approached one of the local farmers and offered to work on the man's farm in exchange for a place to stay and something to eat, and the man was happy to take Ernst-August in.

Peace had come, and except for the fact that he was alone and apart from his family, Ernst-August didn't mind Schlagsdorf. He liked joining the farmer in working the fields, and he loved caring for the animals. He also liked watching the British jeeps drive through the village streets and chatting with the soldiers. Now that the war was over, the soldiers seemed relaxed. They laughed a lot and enjoyed Ernst-August's company. They taught him some English phrases that were new to him, including some words they said he probably shouldn't use in polite company.

On June 17, he celebrated his fifteenth birthday by himself and wondered again what had become of his family. He vowed to do whatever he could to find them. But what could he do? Go back to Neustettin or to Kolberg? Those cities were now in the Russian-occupied territory—what was left of them. If he went there, he would be giving up all of the safety of Schlagsdorf, without any guarantee of finding his family. The best he could think to do, now that Germany had capitulated, would be to find a way back to Ratzeburg, to make contact with anyone who was left from his NSKK unit and see if they might have any knowledge about his family or their whereabouts.

But before Ernst-August could plan this trip, toward the end of June and without warning, the British occupying force told the residents of the village they were enacting a curfew for the next forty-eight hours. No one was permitted to step outside. Ernst-August and the other people of Schlagsdorf heeded the curfew and stayed inside for two days.

When they emerged from their homes, the British soldiers and their jeeps and laughter were gone.

In their place, there were Russian troops everywhere.

Before the end of the war, Roosevelt, Churchill, and Stalin had drawn up a treaty that dictated how they would divide Europe after Germany's inevitable defeat. The treaty included the details for the boundary between west and east—the boundary between the British and Americans on the one side and the Russians on the other.

When the British soldiers arrived in Schlagsdorf in May, they had unknowingly crossed the border dictated by the treaty. They were accidentally occupying Russian territory. The two-day curfew had been put into effect so that the British could evacuate the area and give it over to the Russians in accordance with the treaty.

The people of Schlagsdorf felt betrayed. The British had treated them like friends but had abandoned them without so much as a warning.

Now there was no way for Ernst-August to travel farther west. The Russians quickly constructed a watchtower at the new border and stationed it with armed guards around the clock. The only way across the border was via a bridge at the mouth of Lake Mechow, too close to the watchtower. There was no way for Ernst-August to go west from Schlagsdorf, no way to Ratzeburg.

One afternoon, the Russian commandant in charge of the village showed up outside the farmhouse. "Boy, get the farmer who lives here. I need a horse-drawn carriage and someone to drive it."

They didn't want to make trouble with the Russians, so Ernst-August and the farmer hitched two horses to the carriage and turned it over. "What do you think?" the farmer asked him. "Can you drive him?"

Ernst-August smiled. "I can drive anything."

He had always had a way with animals. He was particularly gifted with horses, and he knew his way around the countryside. But most of all, he knew people. The Russian officers who used the carriage were so quickly and thoroughly charmed by their boy-coachman that they frequently returned and asked him to drive them wherever they needed to go. And always, with a wry smile and a tip of his hat, he obliged. His natural charisma and talents had served him well during the war, and they continued to serve him well after it was over.

Meanwhile, Ernst-August continued working on the farm, wondering about his family but unsure what he could do to find them.

Then, in the first days of December, two young men arrived at the farm one evening, wanting to speak to Ernst-August. They claimed that his father had come to Ratzeburg and would be waiting for him the next morning at the edge of the first village after crossing the border. How was this possible? His father had been in the German army in Italy and was, in all likelihood, a prisoner of war. But even if he was back in Germany, how could he possibly have tracked down Ernst-August in Schlagsdorf? Was this a cruel prank?

But what if it was not a prank? What if his father had indeed been released and had come back to Germany? Could he have made contact with Mr. Schreiber?

He didn't know what to do. The farmer told him absolutely not to risk it. "If the Russians don't shoot you, they will catch you and send you to a work camp in Siberia, and you will never see your family again."

But if it were true, and his father really was waiting on the other side of the border, then Ernst-August knew this might be his only chance to reunite with his family. "I've got to try," he told the farmer.

He woke just before sunrise, grabbed his knapsack, and ran west toward the border until he had a clear view of the Russian watchtower and the bridge. On the other side he saw a small hut he assumed must be manned by British guards.

He prowled along the lakeshore, working his way toward the bridge, hiding among the trees. But he couldn't imagine any way to make it across the long bridge without being seen—and shot—by the Russians.

When he reached the bridge, he went flat on his stomach and started to crawl, pushing his knapsack ahead of him. His progress was unbelievably slow. He was sure that at any moment the guard in the watchtower would see him and shoot. Three-fourths of the way across the bridge, he couldn't crawl anymore, whether from fear or excitement, he didn't know. He jumped up and made a dash for the hut with the British soldiers in it, flying over the gate and literally flinging himself into the arms of the British guards—or so he thought.

The hut was empty.

Was he safe? This was supposed to be the British zone, yet there was no sign of even a single British soldier. He could still see the Russian guard through a hole in the hut. Had he not noticed anything?

Ernst-August would have to make another dash, over the fields, until he reached the woods. He stayed put for several minutes, catching his breath, and then he ran, not stopping until he was in the cover of the trees. From there he found his way to the road that led into the next village.

The Russian guard never even called out.

Far up the road, he could make out the shape of a man walking toward him. It was a shape he would recognize anywhere.

"Dad!" he called out, as he ran up the road. It was his father. Ernst-August could barely believe his eyes. "How did you find me?"

"You're my boy." Ernst threw his arms around his son. "I'll always find you."

The two of them shared a hug while the sun came up. Ernst-August's mind was buzzing with so many questions, he didn't know which one to ask first. Then his father started walking up the road toward Ratzeburg. "Come on," he said.

His father was walking so quickly Ernst-August had difficulty keeping up. "Where are we going?" he asked.

Ernst threw an arm around his boy. "We're going to get your sister. And then all of us are going home."

CHAPTER 28

HAMBURG: 1948

THERE WAS NO MONEY. Technically, that wasn't true. There was *plenty* of money, Reichsmarks left over from Hitler's government. The pieces of paper were everywhere. Everyone had them.

The problem wasn't the lack of money. The problem was that no one wanted it. Since Germany's surrender in 1945, basic services—rations, electricity, and some semblance of law and order—had been provided by the occupying Allies. But there was no real government, and that meant there was nothing backing the old Reichsmark. The currency was worthless paper, and anyone in Germany who had goods or services of any value would not trade those things for worthless paper.

Some basic needs were rationed, but there was no way to shop for additional food or needed supplies.

The people of Germany had escaped the chaos and danger of war only to find themselves in a new kind of chaos: the chaos of poverty, unemployment, and increasing desperation.

Through it all, Ludwig Job continued to go to work. Each morning, he woke in the barracks that his family called home and rode a streetcar through the ruins of Hamburg to arrive at his laboratory at the Philips plant. He worked diligently, putting in long hours, conducting further research to continue to improve radio technology for the company. And at the end of each month, Philips paid him a generous salary—in worthless Reichsmarks.

"We can't go on like this," Ludwig said to his wife one night after the children had gone to sleep. "Month after month, year after year. We need to do something to make it better."

"We're doing fine," Eveline tried to console him. "We're able to put meals on the table."

"Meals?" he argued. "We can't get enough bread with our rationing cards to feed our children. We eat soup every day, but lately it's just turnip soup, again and again turnip soup."

"We eat better than most," she answered him. It was true. Eveline took great pride in her resourcefulness and her ability to provide for her family during these hard times. She was clever, and she knew how to spend her ration coupons for maximum effect, when to barter with friends, and even how to turn to the black market when she had to. Ludwig's words hurt her, even though she knew the two of them wanted the same thing: a good, safe, stable life for their children.

"I work too hard for us to have so little." He looked her in the eye and confided his plan to her. "I think we should move to America. Several of our friends and relatives are doing it."

"America?" Eveline had never heard Ludwig mention such a thing before. "What about your job?"

"What use is a job that pays in worthless money? I'll find a job in America."

"Find a job how? You don't even speak English! None of us do."

"We'll learn."

"Ludwig, you're not a boy anymore. You're not a student."

"I can learn," he insisted. He was confident that he could. Ludwig was already fluent in German and Polish, and he had studied Latin in school. He could pick up another language if he needed to. And he was almost certain that Philips could find a role for him within the company somewhere in America. "It will give us a fresh start."

They went to bed without talking about it any further, but over the next days and weeks, both of them continued to think about America—to wonder if their lives would be better there. Eveline, initially reluctant, began to warm up to the idea. *We would be refugees in America,* she thought. *But we are already refugees. Hamburg isn't our home. Warsaw is our home.*

It was never an option for them to return to Warsaw. Once the Soviets redrew the maps, claiming what had been eastern Poland as part of the USSR and pushing the new western border of Poland into what had been Pomerania, the Polish people had redistributed and settled into their newly reestablished country. It was a country in which Germans were absolutely not tolerated. In the eyes of the Polish, the Germans had caused the war, caused all the dislocation and suffering. Once the borders were redrawn and the Polish government was installed, the remaining Germans in the region, with very few exceptions, were forced to flee west or face robbery, torment, or worse.

The Jobs had been very fortunate, Eveline knew, to find such a safe refuge in Hamburg. But as a family of six they were living in one room in a barrack that they shared with several other families. Now, three years later, they were still cooking rations on a hot plate. It was a hard way to live, and it was a far cry from the life they'd had in Warsaw. This was not a place she particularly thought of as "home."

Maybe Ludwig was right. Maybe America could be that place.

Eveline began studying a map of the United States. It was full of so many unfamiliar place names, and she would pore over the map, trying to understand and imagine a possible life for her family there. One day Elizabeth, by this time ten years of age, caught her with the map. Initially Eveline felt guilty and considered hiding the map from her daughter, the same way they were hiding their plan of possibly moving to America from all their children. No point telling them about it until they had decided for sure.

But then she had a change of heart. Instead of hiding the map, she sat Elizabeth down at the table, and the two of them studied it together. They practiced the foreign names of American states and cities. They turned it into a regular geography lesson and even began quizzing each other.

"Which state is this?" Eveline asked her daughter, pointing to one of the undistinguished squares in the center of the map.

"Colorado," Elizabeth answered quickly. Then she asked her mother, "Do you know the capital of Illinois?"

"Chicago," Eveline guessed. She imagined the faraway city and its majestic buildings looking out onto the giant lake.

"I think the capital of Illinois is Springfield, Mommy."

Elizabeth was a quick study, and she absorbed the contents of the map much faster than Eveline.

"You're right. Chicago is the bigger city, but the capital is Springfield."

Her children would do well in America, Eveline realized. But would she? Would Ludwig? Would their lives there be better? Or worse?

Ludwig kept up his work in the lab, but now, each day, he tried to imagine what it would be like to do the same work in America, in English. Though at first he'd been optimistic, he was starting to have doubts. He would hear the phrases that came out of his mouth during a normal workday—specific, precise, technical phrases, nuanced phrases that came naturally to him thanks to his many years of expertise. *How will I ever learn to say these things in English?*

"Maybe our life here isn't that bad," he conceded to Eveline that night.

"Maybe not," she agreed.

Around Hamburg, day laborers were removing the city's rubble in exchange for food. They cleared the streets to free paths for the trolleys and streetcars and gathered bricks from the bombed-out buildings, piling them up so they could be reused for future building. The city was slowly limping back to life.

The Baptist church on Tresckowstrasse in Hamburg-Eimsbüttel, which had been destroyed and abandoned during the Allied bombing, was rebuilt by volunteers from the congregation in the most simple of ways: by salvaging the ruins and meticulously chipping off the mortar from the old bricks in the rubble, one by one, so they could use the bricks again to erect a new church. The building was a simple structure, without the grandeur of many of Hamburg's older churches, but it offered the Baptist community a renewed sense of sanctuary and hope. Services returned to the rebuilt church, and not long after that Ludwig was chosen as the church elder.

Ludwig and Eveline stopped speaking of America. Their lives were hard, yes, but manageable. Familiar. Ludwig kept going to work each morning. Eveline tended the garden and handled their rations, bartering with their friends and neighbors to make sure they always had what they needed. "One hand," the saying goes, "washes the other."

On June 20, 1948, the German Director of Economics introduced a new currency for Allied-occupied Germany called the Deutschemark. As a part of the planned currency reform, the old, worthless Reichsmarks were gone. Wages were switched to the new currency. Overnight, people throughout the country had the ability to buy and sell again for the first time in years. Bakers started delivering bread, grocers stocked their shelves with food, and construction projects began all over the country.

On payday, Ludwig was given the same amount of money he'd been given before, but now it was in the new currency. Now it had worth. Now he could provide for his family.

Within a few short weeks, the Jobs moved out of the barracks into an apartment in Tresckowstrasse, just across from the Baptist church. It wasn't large or ostentatious, but it was their very own. It had a kitchen and a private bathroom and rooms for the children. Its walls were made of real plaster and not piled-up wardrobes. It had a stove and an oven, not just a hot plate. By year's end three original oil paintings hung on the walls of the living room, just as had been the case in their apartment in Warsaw. The new currency had once again brought business to Hamburg's art galleries.

Once, Ludwig would have taken these amenities for granted. But now he was grateful for them.

Now he was grateful for everything.

CHAPTER 29

((•))

HAMBURG: 1955

SPRINGTIME HAD COME to Hamburg. Rich coral pinks, deep cobalt blues, vermillion reds, and frothy whites—everywhere the cornflowers were abloom, speckling the surrounding hillsides and flushing the city's many parks with color. Along the avenues the magnificent silver birch trees, also known as weeping birches, stood tall and straight. Winter was over, and the trees were no longer weeping; their long, lacy branches budded a delicate green.

The city of Hamburg was not the only thing abloom. As young Friedhelm Radandt walked through the streets, a strange new feeling blossomed in his heart, though he was hesitant to name it.

He was no longer a boy, displaced by war and thrust into the uncertain life of a refugee. Friedhelm was now a man. At twenty-two, he was a university student in Hamburg, the sort of fellow who was curious about everything and never hesitated to ask hard questions. But for once the feeling in his chest had nothing to do with his studies. It was a feeling he was not familiar with, a feeling that could not be subjected to a rubric of academic inquiry.

He stopped at the Alster, the shimmering lake in the heart of the city. It reminded him of sitting in a rowboat with his older brother many years ago on Streitzig Lake. He smiled to think of it. Now, out on the Alster, a young couple was paddling out in a rowboat, a picnic basket wedged between their knees. Friedhelm felt a faint blush rise to his cheeks as he watched them, laughing and flirting in the bashful spring sun. He wouldn't mind having a picnic with a certain girl himself. On the other side of the lake, two boys wobbled on bright yellow bicycles. Friedhelm closed his eyes, remembering.

In the years following World War II, when Germany was still ravaged and slow to recover, times had been hard for the Radandts. There were also wonderful times with their new friends in Nordhorn. The summer Friedhelm was sixteen, he and two of his friends from church spent their vacation on their bikes, pedaling through the country. They traveled for several weeks, often riding sixty or seventy miles a day. They brought a tent with them and set up camp each night in the open meadows.

Friedhelm remembered the trip vividly. They rode as far south as Frankfurt. They rode to the Rhine River and the Köln (Cologne) Cathedral. They saw the damage the war had inflicted upon the country, and they also saw pristine villages and towns that had been left untouched.

One of their stopovers had been in the bombed-out city of Münster, the first place Friedhelm's father had stopped on his trip back from Italy at the end of the war. In Münster, the boys visited the very room where in 1648 the Treaty of Westphalia had been signed, bringing an end to the gruesome Thirty Years' War, a war that had caused terrible suffering and may have wiped out almost one third of Germany's population at the time. It was a bloody conflict that for its reign of unspeakable cruelty had remained fixed in the consciousness of the German people. Pomerania had tasted its horrors to the full. But peace and rebuilding had come to Germany once the treaty had been signed.

Standing in that room in the summer of 1949, almost exactly three centuries later, Friedhelm had a strikingly clear vision of how war seemed to be an ineluctable part of human history. Terrible as it was to admit, there would always be another war, as there would also be a time of restoring and healing the wounds of war.

But what would it take to bring about restoration from the many wounds left by Hitler's war?

Friedhelm spent hours ruminating on this vision, engaging in conversations with anyone he could find. Time and again, he found there wasn't much interest in these sorts of philosophic inquiries. People preferred to reminisce about "old times" and who they had been before the war.

All the more Friedhelm appreciated two of his teachers in Nordhorn who had fought on the eastern front and who openly and willingly talked about their experiences and shared their thoughts with students. Their honesty impressed him, their high regard for human life on either side of the war touched him, and their sorrow over so much evil committed against Jewish people and against those who in the language of the Nazis were deemed "unworthy of life" moved him.

One of those two teachers, Dr. Lichtenberg, first introduced Friedhelm to the concept of actively resisting evil. He told him about the work of Friedrich von Bodelschwingh, a pastor who had refused to tolerate evil when the Nazis came to kill by injection the children with severe mental and physical handicaps under his care. By standing in the doorway and demanding that they kill him first, Pastor von Bodelschwingh saved the lives of those children. Because of this pastor's courage the Nazis did not dare enter the premises he had built to carry out their evil mission there. It was only after the war that the full extent of euthanasia killings ordered by Hitler became known, yet another grim chapter in the history of the Nazi regime.

Friedhelm read up on the details of Pastor Bodelschwingh's story. He wanted to know what had given this man the courage to act on his conscience and where he had found the spiritual strength for his resistance, and he wondered how many others had engaged in active resistance against Hitler. He knew their stories would help young and old come to grips with the reign of terror that had marked the Hitler years and restore the nation's soul.

During these years Friedhelm's thoughts often went back to his home in Pomerania, a landscape of hills, lakes, and forests; to his birthplace Gross-Jestin; and to the beautiful town of Neustettin with its wonderful recreational opportunities. But he knew that the land he remembered so fondly no longer existed. Outwardly it was the same, yet all the residents who had stayed behind during the months of February and March 1945, when the Russian army overran the towns and villages of Pomerania, had been forced to leave their homeland without any of their belongings and settle further west in what had become the Russian zone. Residents of eastern Poland, who had become homeless when their territory was taken over by the Soviet Union, were invited to make Pomerania their homeland. Difficult as it was, it proved to be an action that restored the country of Poland, a land that throughout history had suffered much and which the Nazis had wiped off their maps.

Friedhelm's uncle Max and his family in Gross-Jestin had been among those forced to leave behind their bakery, their home, and all their belongings and become residents of East Germany. There they had to put up with political realities that too often reminded them of the Hitler years. Under Communist rule, private bakeries were forbidden. Max would never again own his own business, though he did bookwork for a large, group-owned bakery. But he continued to play the organ at church, and that was far more important to him than owning an oven or baking bread. He had found a community, a place to call home. Friedhelm's cousins discovered they were now required to join and regularly attend a Communist youth organization. The flag was different, as were the uniforms, but the discipline and the training reminded them of the Hitlerjugend.

While Friedhelm in Nordhorn enjoyed freedom, his cousins in the Russian zone once again lived under a system of oppressive government. But he was unable to visit them because travel from West to East or vice versa generally was not allowed, even though some managed to escape through the Iron Curtain and find freedom in the western zones. The East–West division remained entrenched for decades, a visible marker that pointed to a great need: restoring Germany from the wickedness of the Hitler regime and the destruction the war had left.

It wasn't just the East–West division, a division that separated the two Germanys and also separated eastern from western Europe, that made spiritual and political renewal difficult. For years, Friedhelm and his generation had to deal with the constant reports about the holocaust, the gradual revelation of a genocidal evil committed against the Jewish people that was of much greater proportions and immensity than they could have imagined. They had to find answers, and they would ask pointed questions of the older generation.

A slight breeze whipped across the lake, and Friedhelm pulled his jacket closer as he turned away and continued his walk. It may have been spring, but there was still a nip of winter in the air.

It had been a full decade since he had seen Streitzig Lake or set foot in Neustettin. Friedhelm had come to Hamburg in 1954. His studies at the university were stimulating and engaging, and he loved his new home. Of course, the city still showed the marks of severe war damage, but already the downtown had been almost entirely rebuilt. The streets were gleaming with new buildings. The neighborhood of Hammerbrook had been reinvented as a thriving shopping district, and nearby Rothenburgsort was in the midst of a similar renovation. New apartment buildings and houses were popping up all over the city. It was truly invigorating to live in the midst of such a vibrant rebirth.

Like his parents before him, Friedhelm began looking for a Baptist fellowship as soon as he arrived in Hamburg. This had, after all, been his family's saving grace: no matter where they settled they had never been truly alone, because they always established ties to the nearest Baptist community. Friedhelm, too, sought to put down roots in a local Baptist church. During his early days in Hamburg, he devoted quite a bit of time to researching the various locations and debating the options with his new friends. After much discussion, he decided to take a closer look at the Baptist Church on Tresckowstrasse, in Hamburg-Eimsbüttel.

He was richly rewarded. At the church, Friedhelm found the kind of fellowship that appealed to him—so much so that he felt at home right from the start. The unimpeachable integrity of the pastor, Reverend Herbert Wieske, appealed to him. One of the best-known stories about Reverend Wieske was that a British commando had turned to this pastor for counsel and advice after the war, and young Friedhelm could see why.

Hamburg proved to be the city where he would continue delving into the most recent past of Germany, including the role of the Baptist denomination during the Nazi regime. Friedhelm became fascinated to learn about those in Nazi Germany who in one form or another had stood up against the evil being perpetrated. They were pastors and priests, officers in the military, teachers, writers, scholars, civil servants, and political activists. Their number likely reached over forty thousand, and the vast majority of them died in prison and in concentration camps or were executed. What had driven these men and women to take the first step toward resistance? Most often it was that they decided to let their conscience speak. And what had wounded their consciences most often were the Nazi laws against Jews. One of the most outstanding pastors of the resistance had been Dietrich Bonhoeffer. His writings left a deep impact on Friedhelm.

In Hamburg, Friedhelm participated actively in the Baptist student chapter at the university, and the topic of the holocaust and of resistance came up in their meetings. They wondered aloud why they had never heard of anyone in the leadership of their denomination in Germany playing a part in standing up against Hitler and his policies publicly, and why some of them on occasion had even worn Nazi uniforms. They were pleased when some of those who had filled responsible positions during the Nazi era were willing to meet with them. Their answers, however, left the group of students bewildered. What Friedhelm and his fellow Baptist students heard was that in contrast to the Weimar Republic with its financial havoc, Hitler early on had stabilized Germany's economic climate and won the trust of many. That answer, while true, did not address the question of evil that lurked behind the Aryan rules, or the terror tactics that from the start shaped Hitler's murderous actions against the Jewish people, or even Hitler's plan to make the church an Aryan German church that would have to give up on the Old Testament.

As Friedhelm continued reading about those heroes of the faith who had been involved in the struggle of resistance, and as he immersed himself in Dietrich Bonhoeffer's *Ethics,* he concluded that he had to talk about the issue of resistance to Baptist young people's groups. He would include excerpts from Hitler's speeches and cite prison and death sentences pronounced by judges in Hitler's courtrooms. And he would give short summaries of the acts of resistance. After one such talk in the city of Kiel, where the group of young people had been particularly large, a Baptist pastor came over to express his support. He agreed that dealing with the past was important for any people, but especially so for people of faith. Doing so frees them to do God's work with integrity. Friedhelm was thankful and encouraged.

His time at the church on Tresckowstrasse had brought him much more than he ever imagined. Yes, it had provided a warm and supportive community, countless wise teachings, and friendship with its pastor, a tremendous man of faith. And yet, as Friedhelm that spring day walked under the blossoming trees, his mind was drawn in an entirely different direction. He was thinking of a much younger member of the congregation, someone he had met in the weekly young-adult circle meetings—a young woman he had begun to look for at every church-related gathering.

He was thinking of Elizabeth Job.

((ᛘ))

Friedhelm was not the only one out for a walk in Hamburg on that brisk spring day. Elizabeth Job was now a winsome young woman of seventeen, and on her way home from work she enjoyed a walk along Alster Lake before catching the streetcar that would take her to Niendorf. She too had noticed the young couple shyly picnicking in their rowboat, and she couldn't help but let out a wistful sigh.

The church on Tresckowstrasse had been very good to the Job family. The Jobs had been attending services regularly ever since arriving in Hamburg in 1945, and in that time they had become one of the most active families in the congregation. Ludwig served as the ruling elder, and Georg, Eduard, and Elizabeth were a regular part of the young-adult circle.

A smile played at the corners of Elizabeth's mouth. Over the last few months, the young-adult circle had fast become her favorite part of going to church. The lessons were wonderful and thought provoking, but that wasn't the thing that made her heart beat a little bit faster every time she took her place in the circle.

There was a new face in the group, a slender, serious young student from Nordhorn, who had captured her attention from the very first day he'd come to church. She could still remember sitting with her family, earnestly trying to focus on Reverend Wieske's sermon but feeling a very strong temptation to crane her neck and look at the handsome young man in the next pew.

Unbidden, Elizabeth began humming the melody of a lullaby as she walked.

Maikäfer flieg!
Der Vater ist im Krieg
Die Mutter ist im Pommerland
Und Pommerland ist abgebrannt
Maikäfer flieg!

It was strange that she even knew this lullaby, considering she'd spent her early years—the years when her mother would have sung her lullabies—in Poland. But in the years since the war, the song had become more prevalent, not just in Pomerania but in all of Germany. The lullaby had broad appeal because "Pommerland" had begun to stand for everybody's homeland, whether it was Pomerania or Westphalia, Germany or Poland.

A *Maikäfer* was like a June bug, a pest native to Pomerania. Ever since she'd heard that Friedhelm Radandt hailed originally from Pomerania, she had not been able to get the tune out of her head.

June bug, fly!
The father is in the war.
The mother is in Pommerland,
Pommerland is burnt down.
June bug, fly!

Sometimes the lullaby made Elizabeth unspeakably sad. A father goes off to the war, the mother stays behind, and their home in Pomerania burns to the ground. While her own home had not burned to the ground, she knew well the feeling of being displaced. She was, after all, a refugee from Poland, never to return to her childhood home.

After the barracks, the Jobs had moved into an apartment close to Elizabeth's school for a year. Then, in 1949, they purchased a house in the beautiful residential area of Hamburg-Niendorf, their first real home since fleeing Warsaw four years before. Elizabeth loved the house, loved her own room, and loved the opportunity to decorate it to her taste. Hamburg truly had become home to her and her brothers, and hope was in the air.

Still, Elizabeth thought often of those three years during which, as a family of six, they had lived in that one room in the barracks near the Hamburg Tierpark. Those times spent playing and learning with her family had left indelible memories in her mind.

Her father's birthday was December 18, and each year they invited church friends and friends from their days in Poland over for a celebration. They would light candles, and in the warm candlelight everything looked prettier, and no one paid any attention to the bare surroundings of their refugee existence. Instead, they saw happy faces crowded around a table, eating cake and laughing. The house was flooded with singing and togetherness, and later on in the evening, if there were newcomers, her father would retell the story of their journey from Poland—a story he never tired of telling, of one miracle after another.

Those years were also the time when Ludwig learned the news of his three brothers, news that made its way to Hamburg only gradually. He had grown up with them on the family farm in Gross-Grabina, and all three of them had been drafted into the war and sent to the Eastern Front. None of the three had survived the war. Their lives were snuffed out on the battlefield, and their sons would grow up fatherless.

Now that she was old enough to have a job, Elizabeth was happy to be interning at Philips. It gave her somewhere to go every day and work that engaged her. She proudly made her way to the stately Philips building, which had never been marred by the bombing. The building was only one block from the main rail station, which had been heavily damaged. On her walks to and from work, Elizabeth often peeked in at the station, which was once again topped by a resplendent glass dome. The dome had thousands of tiny windowpanes, and for years she watched the workmen replace each individual pane until they had repaired the whole edifice. It made her spirit soar to see the men meticulously restoring the train station to its original beauty.

Elizabeth picked up her pace, eager to get home and change out of her office attire, eat dinner, and go to sleep. She had church in the morning, and she wanted to be well rested so she would look sharp. She didn't want to admit it to herself, but she hoped very much that Friedhelm Radandt would be there. It was a rare Sunday when he wasn't.

Elizabeth couldn't explain it exactly, but she felt, in a way, that her life story had been drawing her ever closer to Friedhelm—that their destinies were soon to be intertwined.

Sometimes when she thought these things, she brushed them off as the idle fantasies of a silly schoolgirl. But sometimes she felt that Friedhelm's arrival in Hamburg was not coincidence. Nor was it fate, because Elizabeth did not believe in such a thing.

What she believed in was the hand of God.

EPILOGUE

((ı))

HAMBURG AND BEYOND: 1955–1960

IT DIDN'T TAKE Friedhelm and Elizabeth long to realize their attraction was mutual.

Whenever Friedhelm spoke in the young-adult circle at church, Elizabeth listened attentively. Whenever Elizabeth walked into the church on Sunday mornings, Friedhelm sat up a little straighter in his pew. As they learned more about one another and their respective families, a mutual respect and admiration began to grow.

Then, one day in late spring 1955, the young-adult circle broached a new topic: people's lives before the war. Each person in the meeting talked about the war and their unique experience of it. Friedhelm and Elizabeth both sat in amazement as they listened to one another, marveling at the marked similarities between their two stories, the dramatic highs and lows of their lives as refugees.

The conversation was so lively, it didn't stop when the meeting was over. Friedhelm walked out with Elizabeth, still talking, their conversation carrying the two of them down the steps of the church and out onto the sidewalk.

"Oh my," Elizabeth said, checking the time. "I promised to be home for dinner. I don't want to stop talking, but I'm afraid I'll miss my streetcar."

"May I accompany you?" Friedhelm blurted, hoping he wasn't being too forward. "If I walk you to the stop, we can keep talking."

She smiled. "I'd like that very much."

Together they strolled to the stop. It was a fifteen-minute walk from the church, but for both of them it seemed to pass in seconds. The conversation flowed freely as they discovered more and more things they had in common. They exchanged bits and pieces about their families, backgrounds, and interests. Neither could deny that the world seemed to take on a certain sparkle as they talked. All around them the flowers were blooming and the birds were crooning in the silver birch trees. Hamburg had sprung to life—and their hearts beat a little faster.

When the #2 streetcar arrived, ready to carry Elizabeth to her home in Hamburg-Niendorf, they were both reluctant to say good-bye. So they let the first streetcar pass. Then the second. When Elizabeth finally climbed onboard the #2, both she and Friedhelm were flushed with the potential of the obvious bond between them.

"This has been so lovely," she gushed. "I hope . . . I'd truly like to do it again."

Amazed at her own audacity, Elizabeth turned around and hurried onto the streetcar before Friedhelm could formulate a reply. She stared out the window, aflutter with excitement, watching as Friedhelm got smaller and smaller through the glass. She knew he usually caught the streetcar at a stop only a block away from the church and that it spirited him away to Hamburg-Horn at the opposite end of the city. He had gone out of his way! He had accompanied her to the streetcar stop in front of all her friends—a welcome signal to her. It was as if he'd made a conscious public statement of his interest. Though Elizabeth was a sensible girl, she couldn't help but be flattered.

Friedhelm, for his part, couldn't believe the strange things that were happening with time. How could the time have passed so quickly? He decided to walk to Dammtorbahnhof, where he'd catch the streetcar to Hamburg-Horn. The whole time, thoughts of his all-too-short conversation with Elizabeth were spinning in his mind. Though they had lingered a good while after the circle meeting, the time had passed far too swiftly. He'd never felt this sort of connection before, not with anyone. Why did it have to end?

When he climbed onto the streetcar half an hour later, he avidly began making plans to invite Elizabeth on their first real date.

As the car hurtled toward the dormitory where Friedhelm lived, he remained lost in his thoughts, replaying the many events that tied him and Elizabeth together. As children, they had both narrowly escaped the Russians and been peacefully liberated by the British and Canadian troops. Of course, there were differences too. Elizabeth had confessed that she still woke from dreams about devastating bombardments. During her years in Hamburg, she had spent many nights in bomb shelters, whereas Friedhelm had never spent a single night in an air raid underground. She had even seen the Jewish ghetto in Warsaw, before her family was forced to flee. She admitted it was hard for her to talk about what she had seen, hard to discuss the atrocities that had been committed. Friedhelm realized that except for Kristallnacht in Neustettin, when he had walked over broken glass on a sidewalk, he had never encountered atrocities against the Jews. It occurred to him too that unlike the Jobs in Hamburg, his experience had been one of peaceful and free living once the family managed to get out of Kolberg. How different their adventures had been before and during that terrible war, and yet how similar their stories were in so many ways.

Now, with the war behind them, there was an opportunity for a new beginning. Friedhelm tried not to get ahead of himself, but he couldn't help but dream about what might come. He had admired Elizabeth for quite some time, the feelings blossoming quietly in his chest. And now he had proof—real proof!—that his feelings were reciprocated. How special would it be to start a new life with Elizabeth Job, to build a marriage on such a powerful common experience? How wonderful would it be to create a future together, maybe even in America?

Friedhelm had spent some time in the United States, and the American dream loomed large in his heart. He was drawn to the land of opportunity. He imagined a life for himself and Elizabeth where they could raise a family in a country far from home.

In the years since the war, Friedhelm had come to see his own story and that of his family as nothing less than a set of miracles. How else had they escaped the war safely and found one another in the end?

Now here was Elizabeth, whose own story was also a set of miracles. And they had found each other in Hamburg, a city of which neither of them was a native. If not for the war, Elizabeth would still be in Poland, and Friedhelm might have been back in Pomerania, collecting June bugs and letting them fly while singing a sad lullaby.

On her streetcar home, Elizabeth was thinking much the same thing.

Her heart was full of gratitude. On that spring day, each of them had been touched by the other's gestures of love—a word that had not yet been spoken aloud but had been brewing in both their hearts for quite some time. It was clear to Elizabeth and Friedhelm that an authentic romance had started to bud. And that romance would blossom into a deep, abiding love indeed.

Over the next three years, Friedhelm and Elizabeth took long walks along the Elbe River and through the hilly forests of Hamburg-Harburg. They went to concerts and picnics, and of course they saw each other regularly at church. Friedhelm was soon invited as a regular Sunday dinner guest at the Job house, where the issues of the day were discussed around the dinner table. Ludwig never missed an opportunity to engage in intellectual discussions. This was, after all, what he most liked to do. After the meal, Ludwig would often pick up *Die Welt,* the famous Hamburg newspaper, hand it to Friedhelm, and say, "Why don't you read this editorial?" Once Friedhelm had read it, they would enthusiastically discuss it, along with all the other members of the Job family.

The Jobs discussed politics like a modern-day American family might discuss sports: sure, they might argue about the different parties, but nobody got angry with one another, even if they disagreed. With Friedhelm at the table, they discussed all the major issues of the day, and it made Elizabeth's father very happy that her suitor could hold his own in these stimulating debates.

As Friedhelm's student years in Hamburg came to an end, he was asked to serve on the board of the Hamburg Youth Council (the Hamburger Jugendring), a group dedicated to ensuring that in this postwar era, all youth organizations in the city adhered to democratic principles. Friedhelm's special role was to represent the youth of all the Baptist churches in Hamburg as well as those of several other free churches.

The assignment made him think more about the need to stand up for freedom, and his interest in resistance work during World War II grew. He began to read avidly about the heroes in the German resistance movement against Hitler, wanting to understand what had made them stand up against Nazi ideology and Nazi rule. He wanted to know why some men and women were willing to give their lives for their convictions.

Elizabeth was haunted by her own memories, particularly of the little girl getting kicked back under the fence of the Jewish ghetto in Warsaw. And there were other, more horrible things she had not seen but that haunted her still. "My aunt told me about the trains going to Treblinka," she told Friedhelm, the color draining from her face. "They shoved dozens of them in and slammed the doors shut on them like they were cattle."

Friedhelm nodded vehemently. She was putting into words something he had so often felt. Though many Germans were willing and even eager to talk about their own experiences during the war, far fewer of them wanted to discuss what had been done to the Jews—and whether they themselves were implicated in the Holocaust.

After he was asked to serve on the Hamburg Youth Council, Friedhelm devoted a great deal of time and energy to exploring these questions. One of the projects the council undertook was to organize a bus trip that brought thousands of young people from both Hamburg and Berlin to the Bergen-Belsen death camp. Together they observed a day of remembrance.

At Bergen-Belsen, the young Germans stood in silence, staring at the multiple mass graves. A girl began crying softly. Others shook their heads, while many clasped their hands together in silent prayer. The graves were horrifying and nauseating—no words could describe the atrocities that had been committed on that site.

"How could this happen?" the youth asked Friedhelm on the bus ride back as they attempted to fathom the scale of what had happened.

But Friedhelm challenged them to think another, harder thought. "How could we do this?" he asked them. "Why didn't we stop it?"

They argued with him. "We were too young!" they said. "We were children. We didn't know. Some of us weren't even born. We would never do something like this."

Friedhelm could tell they meant what they said, but he also knew that most of their parents would probably have said the same thing. Yet that hadn't kept the Holocaust from happening. He thought about his own father, who in the late 1930s had made the conscious decision to follow God and the Bible in the face of Nazi pressure, come what may. It was that decision that later gave Ernst the courage to refuse the offer the Nazis made on the front steps of their house in Neustettin, when they invited Friedhelm to join the special Nazi training school. A deep sense of gratitude overcame him as he thought of it.

How was Friedhelm to answer these youths on the bus? Was there even an answer? He knew that, during the war, people had made their own decisions, had drawn their own line between what was right and what was wrong, and too many of them—too many of *us*, Friedhelm corrected himself—too many of us drew that line in a place that fell far short of right. There are those who consistently do the right thing by their friends, neighbors, and family, yet even their line falls short when their sense of impartiality succumbs to propaganda or to personal dislikes.

That's when they suddenly disown neighbors, friends, or even family members whom they are told to hate.

And Friedhelm quoted the sobering sentence that had stood out in the speeches that day at Bergen-Belsen, spoken by someone too young to have fought in the war:

"If our parents could do it, then we could do it too."

He wanted to encourage people to do better. The memory of Bergen-Belsen weighed heavily on those young minds on the bus, irrefutable proof that faith in humanity is often misplaced. Now that they were on their way home, Friedhelm wanted them to see the other side of that sobering statement—to heed the call of their parents and grandparents who did the *right* thing during the war.

Friedhelm had met many people who believed the war had brought them closer to the Lord. They had witnessed the horrible cruelties people inflicted upon one another and the unstoppable, uncontrollable power of evil. Once they understood this, they were able to see, hidden amidst the tragedies and atrocities of the war, thousands of stories of people who had been guided on their paths and protected by God.

That was one of the greatest lessons he had learned from the war: that the humanity in people could and would flourish, even under the direst of circumstances. Both his family and Elizabeth's had been touched, over and over, by the kindness of the people God had put in their paths. Countless men and women had offered them food, lodging, friendship, and safety. They had come through the war with their families intact. They had survived and flourished, paving the way for new lives and loves to be forged.

((ı))

After dating for three years, Friedhelm and Elizabeth's commitment to one another deepened beyond their highest expectations. Their relationship confirmed, again and again, that love can be a beautiful and mutual thing. They felt the support of the Job family in Hamburg and the Radandt family in Nordhorn, and wedding bells were ringing louder and louder in their ears. More importantly, they felt a kinship they knew would last over the years.

On June 16, 1958, Elizabeth and Friedhelm said "I do" in the Baptist church of Hamburg-Eimsbüttel. It was the church where they had first met, a church literally rebuilt from the rubble of World War II, standing strong on its ancient foundation. In some ways, their marriage was like that, too—a partnership built on the foundation of two refugee stories, both tales of faith, courage, hardship, hope, and survival.

Both families had fled the violence of war. Their safety and comfort had been stripped from them, their plans and dreams irrevocably altered. They had lost their homes and their histories in the rubble left by a vile dictator, the rubble of vainglory and genocide and mass destruction. Their lives had been forever marred by the ugliness of war.

In January of 1960, Friedhelm and Elizabeth immigrated to America, arriving in New York City aboard the SS *United States*.

Their old journey had come to an end.

Their new journey had just begun.

ACKNOWLEDGMENTS

BREE BARTON WAS my writing partner. It was she who, through her inquisitive questioning, unearthed the storyline that fused the tales of two families into one. Most importantly, it was she whose knack for highlighting the dramatic parts of the story made this book a page-turner. If there is value in these pages for today's reader, the credit goes to her. From the start, Bree considered it a pleasure to work on this book.

Thank you to Kit Tosello and to Andy Carmichael, both at Deep River Books, who made the publishing process easy and satisfying. Many thanks are due my editor, Rachel Starr-Thompson, who mingled words of praise with just the right questions to show more clearly aspects of the human conscience in conflict.

Still, this book would never have become reality had it not been for the constant support I received from my wife, Elizabeth. She has brought abiding love and joy into our marriage, and her part in the story adds immeasurably to the perspective that puts personal experiences into a historical setting. To her I owe deep gratitude. She is a daily reminder of the life-shaping influence those war years had on her and on me, truly making it our story.

Nor would this book have been written without the strong encouragement from my son, André, who, having heard the story repeatedly in his early years, envisioned it being told to a much wider audience. I am also indebted to my daughter, Dorit, who urged me on in the genealogical family research that was needed to understand how and why our two families had come to live where they were living at the start of the Hitler years and what had given them such strong faith, strong enough to say no at crucial times to Nazi demands.

Years ago, I asked my dad to write down for me what he knew of the Radandt family history. Upon his death, I became the recipient of the various documents he collected, including the unfinished original of the Aryan purity questionnaire that he was asked to submit to the Party. My brother wrote down for me his experiences during the last few months of World War II, and my sister Brunhild related conversations she had with my mother about details of our escape that were unknown to me. My cousin Manfred Rattunde was always ready to answer my questions and send documents to support his recollection of his war experiences. I also heard from Elizabeth's dad the story of their escape from Poland and of his work in the underground laboratory. Then there was the transcript of a talk her brother Eduard gave at a family gathering, containing many details that helped me piece the story together, and the many documents about the family that her brother Georg had assembled. Elizabeth's cousins, Welli Wenzel and Inka Rahn, gladly responded to my questions, as did her aunt and uncle Lilly and Waldemar Giesbrecht. To all of them I express my gratitude.

Finally, I owe thanks to many friends and family members who kept urging me on. They are too numerous to mention by name.

DISCUSSION QUESTIONS

Chapter 1

1. Why did Hitler's advisors, at a time when the war seemed all but lost, urge the Führer to address the German nation after a long pause of speaking publicly? What was the occasion, and what did they hope to achieve?

2. How did the Nazi programs that Hitler developed for young people affect the lives of the two older children in the Radandt household?

3. In what ways should we consider the situation in which the Radandt family finds itself toward the end of the war as typical, and in which ways is it unique?

Chapter 2

1. Does it surprise us to meet in the Jobs a German refugee family from Poland? Why?

2. How is it possible for Ludwig Job, as a refugee, to be more up-to-date than most about the troop movements in the east?

3. What are the factors that influence the Jobs to choose Hamburg as their next destination? What gives them the luxury of choosing?

Chapter 3

1. What attracted Ernst Radandt to work part-time for Strength through Joy, and what were the goals of this organization?

2. What do you think of Hitler's usage of the word "Volk" (meaning "the people") in such combinations as "Volksempfänger" and "Volkswagen" and "Volksdeutsch"? What did he want to accomplish?

3. What factors contributed to Ernst's decision not to submit the ancestry table to prove his Aryan purity?

Chapter 4

1. What role did the German-speaking Baptist churches in Poland play in the lives of the Job and Witt families?

2. How did the Job and Witt families manage their dual loyalties as Polish citizens and as members of the Protestant German community in Poland?

3. Given that Ludwig was a Polish citizen and had no personal connections to anyone in Germany, what would he have known about Nazi practices prior to the German occupation of Poland?

Chapter 5

1. What necessitated the move of the Radandt family from Gross-Jestin to Neustettin?

2. How did Ernst escape the revenge of the Nazis just prior to the war? What does that say about the relationship between the military and the Party under Nazi rule?

3. Name the factors that contributed to a largely normal life for the Radandts in Neustettin before and after the start of the war.

Chapter 6

1. What made the September 1, 1939, German invasion so unsettling for the German community in Poland?

2. How did having a son and a brother as an officer in the Polish army affect the Witt and Job families in Warsaw?

3. What changes did the German occupation of Warsaw bring to the Philips plant in that city?

Chapter 7

1. What do you think of Hitler's decision to change the common script from Gothic to Roman in the middle of a war? Why did Germany continue using Roman writing after the war?

2. Did the many victory newsbreaks on the radio give the German population a sense of confidence in the Führer? What does this say about Hitler's decision early on to increase the number of radios in German homes?

3. What does the story of Ernst Radandt's encounter with the forester tell you?

Chapter 8

1. What factors might have contributed to Bruno Witt's enlisting in the Polish army? What does that say about his love for the country?

2. How did "Volksdeutsche" in Warsaw experience life under the German occupation? How was it different for Polish nationals?

3. How does Ludwig, living in Poland where his ancestors had lived for six generations, feel about being given German citizenship papers by the occupation forces?

Chapter 9

1. What made eastern Pomerania a safe place for evacuees from the industrial Ruhr district in the west?

2. Consider how a Christian grandfather touches the life of a questioning grandson.

3. How did the two Radandt boys get their first skis in the middle of the war? What does their experience say about the harbingers of a crushing end to the war?

Chapter 10

1. Why did the experience at the fence of the Warsaw Ghetto leave such a lasting impression in five-year-old Elizabeth's mind?

2. What possible connection does Ludwig see between the Warsaw Ghetto and his sister Olga's story of a transport taking Jews to Treblinka? How does it affect him?

3. How was Ludwig Job able to make the lives of his Polish coworkers a bit easier during the German occupation? What motivated him?

Chapter 11

1. What might have motivated Ernst and Gertrud to hold regular prayer and Bible study meetings in their home? And what might the attendees have gained from being part of this house church?

2. What gave Ernst the courage to refuse the request to enroll his sons at the Nazi training school?

3. What does Ernst's being assigned to a military office job in Italy at a time when the eastern front was collapsing say about the power the Nazis had over the army?

Chapter 12

1. What are the various changes that Ludwig and his family have to deal with in 1944?

2. What does the huge project in the abandoned mine of Porta Westfalica say about the status of the war, and why does Ludwig stay to himself as much as possible except for participation in the church?

3. Why, when they must escape danger from the Polish resistance in Warsaw, do Ludwig and Eveline choose Kalisz, a town within the former borders of Poland, rather than going to Germany proper?

Chapter 13

1. How does Gertrud Radandt cope with the fear of the Russian invasion? How does she deal with having two of her children taken from her custody? Did she have a choice in losing her children?

2. What kind of questions does the Ostwall project raise in the minds of people generally, and Gertrud particularly?

3. What thoughts go through Ernst-August's mind when he hears over the radio of the failed assassination on Hitler's life?

Chapter 14

1. What things cast a glow over a very dark Christmas in Kalisz in 1944?

2. Why can both Eveline in Kalisz and Gertrud in Neustettin feel assured that their husbands are quite safe in their respective locations at a time when so many face mortal danger on the battlefield?

3. What role does the church play in the life of the Job family?

Chapter 15

1. What effect might the failed assassination have had on Hitler's mind and on his determination to keep the war machine going?

2. What drove Ludwig on January 20, 1945, to leave his job unauthorized and take the train to Kalisz?

3. Why would Eveline call her January 21, 1945 birthday "the best ever"?

Chapter 16

1. Why did being left behind in Neustettin bother Friedhelm considerably less than it did his mother?

2. What does it say about the Nazi image and tactics when we learn of a Latvian SS troop assigned to defend Neustettin?

3. How do we explain Ernst-August's refusal to listen to his mother's pleas and leave his NSKK unit?

Chapter 17

1. Why was the decision to vacate Kalisz given so late? And why was the decision made not to defend the town?

2. Crossing the border from Poland into Germany elicits emotional responses. How are the responses from the Job children different from those of their parents?

3. All by himself on a flat freight car, Ludwig is overcome with a sense of great thankfulness. What is behind this emotion?

Chapter 18

1. Friedhelm's going back to their house to pick up his father's suitcase meant that the family would now have a sled. Why was that important, and what does it say about God's protective guidance?

2. How does the German army plan to defend Kolberg, and how does Friedhelm find out about it?

3. How do Gertrud and Friedhelm learn that the siege of Kolberg has started?

Chapter 19

1. What made Ludwig decide that they needed to cross the Oder River if they wanted to be safe from the Russian army?

2. What is the housing situation in Hamburg at the beginning of 1945, and why is it likely to get worse?

3. What is required of a family like the Jobs to establish residency in Hamburg so that they will receive food-rationing cards?

Chapter 20

1. What thoughts does the description of the serenity of life at the Rittergut Dolgen awake in you?

2. Describe the fear that had the Schützes and Gisela cross the lake with its ice cover buried underneath a layer of slush.

3. How did the unlikely encounter between the two siblings on the east Pomeranian escape route affect their minds and what information were they able to exchange?

Chapter 21

1. What parallel does Eveline draw in her mind between the city of Hamburg in ruins and her own family?

2. How does the church in bomb-charred Hamburg meet the needs of the Jobs?

3. What role do dolls play in young Elizabeth's life, and in what way do they symbolize the horror of war?

Chapter 22

1. From Friedhelm's perspective, what did the face of death look like in Kolberg under siege?

2. How did Friedhelm's grandfather become a symbol of strength for him?

3. Why did the look back at Kolberg from the deck of the freighter remain permanently etched in Friedhelm's memory?

Chapter 23

1. What brought the constant air raids over Hamburg to an end?

2. What feelings did the announcement of Hitler's death arouse in Eveline?

3. What did the announcement do to Ludwig?

Chapter 26

1. How did what Friedhelm experienced and observed from aboard the freighter as it was moving west satisfy his curiosity and fill him with new hope?

2. What made Easter 1945 such a joyous experience for Friedhelm and to a degree even for his mother?

3. What made being liberated by the British and Canadian forces such a satisfying event?

Chapter 25

1. How did the culturally diverse expertise that the Rosners exhibited keep their families safe when the Russian tanks arrived in Bärwalde?

2. What are your thoughts as you reflect on the daring and highly adventurous experiment the Rosners undertook when the war was surely lost and the future uncertain?

3. How does one's deep-rooted familiarity with one's mother tongue affect at least two instances in the Rosner story?

Chapter 26

1. In what way was the dream about Ernst's coming home to Nordhorn a gracious touch from God on the series of miracles that happened to make his return possible?

2. What might have prompted the Jewish officer in the US Army to send Ernst home?

3. How must Gertrud have felt when Ernst could tell her that Gisela and the Schützes had safely made it into the west?

Chapter 27

1. What thoughts might have gone through Ernst-August's mind when he secretly threw away his uniform and put on the civilian clothes his mother had given him several months earlier?

2. What do you make of Ernst's wanting Friedhelm to understand that Germany's defeat was a sign of God's grace? Can there be grace in defeat?

3. What jarring experience does the end of the war bring to Ernst-August and the residents of Schlagsdorf?

Chapter 28

1. What helped the Jobs to survive their one-room living arrangement in the barrack for three years?

2. How was it possible for a new currency to jumpstart the economy virtually overnight?

3. What motivated the folks of the Baptist church in Hamburg Eimsbüttel to rebuild with their own hands a sanctuary from the ruins the bombs had left?

Chapter 29

1. What questions flooded Friedhelm's mind when in 1949 he visited the very room in which the Westphalian Peace Treaty had been signed three hundred years earlier?

2. In what major ways did the people in East Germany continue to live under oppressive totalitarianism? In which ways was that the opposite of life in West Germany?

3. How did Friedhelm become aware of people who resisted Hitler's euthanasia program and his policies against the Jewish people? What did he do with that information?

Epilogue

1. Where did Friedhelm and Elizabeth first meet, and how did they find out about each other's refugee experiences?

2. What was Friedhelm's part in planning a huge gathering of young people at the site of the Bergen-Belsen concentration camp, and what question in particular did he want young people to consider?

3. In what ways did the war experiences bring people closer to God?

The Rattunde family

Opa Rattunde as a WWI soldier in Metz (France) with his prayer team. The words “God is Love” are captured on the photo.

The newlyweds, Ernst and Gertrud, enjoy motorcycle rides.

Der Regierungspräsident

Ernst Radandt

Ernst Radandt’s driver’s license, issued in 1926. Initially limited to motorcycles, it was later extended to automobiles. This driver’s license served him for the rest of his life.

Julius and Eugenia Witt, Elizabeth’s maternal grandparents, during their early years of marriage.

Eveline Job, Elizabeth's mother, during her student days in Warsaw.

Ludwig Job, the young physicist, working for Philips in Warsaw.

The Witt-Job family home in Wlochy, near Warsaw, where all four Job children were born. The brick fence and gate were added after the war.

Ahnentafel

Ahnentafel:

The official genealogical table on which Ernst Radandt was to document his Aryan descent.

The Radandt family in 1943, with Gisela, Ernst-August, and Friedhelm standing behind their parents and Brunhild.

Ludwig and Eveline Job on a stroll in Warsaw in the early 1940s.

The Job children in 1942: Eduard, Georg, Elizabeth, and Waldemar.

Julius and Eugenia Witt in Lodz, listening to the sounds of their newest Philips radio. With them are Elizabeth's uncle Richard Witt and aunt Lilly Job.

Mainly the younger crowd of the Radandt house church in Neustettin, with Ernst-August (shortly before he was drafted into the military), Brunhild, and Friedhelm in front center.

Fourteen-year-old Bubi (Ernst-August) as a soldier in the NSKK.

Ernst-August (front left) with his NSKK unit outside the military barracks in Neustettin.

A postcard Friedhelm sent from Kolberg on the 17th of February, 1945, to his brother who was stationed with his military unit in Neustettin.

Friedhelm's grandparents in Kolberg toward the end of WWII.

Elizabeth doing homework in the Job family's one-room refugee living space in the barracks in Hamburg. As usual, she had brought in a bouquet of wildflowers to spruce up the place.

Moving day for the Job family in 1948, when they could at last leave the barracks. Elizabeth's uncle Richard gave the Job children a ride in the two-wheeled wagon they'd used to transport their few belongings.

Left: Friedhelm in the United States, in 1953.

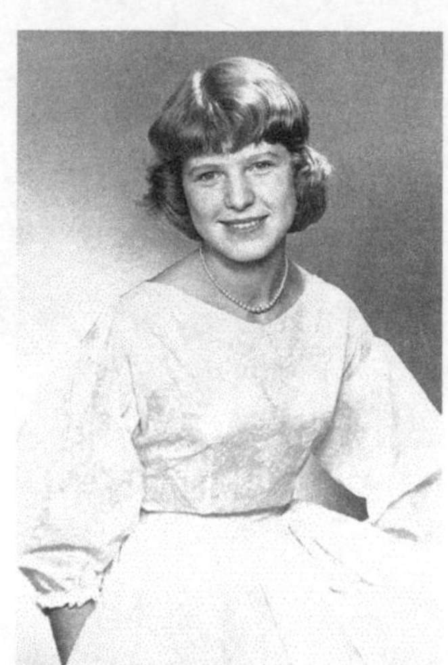

Right: Elizabeth in Hamburg, in 1957.

Above: Friedhelm and Elizabeth at the occasion of their engagement.

Left: Friedhelm and Elizabeth, surrounded by their families, boarding the SS United States in January 1960.